THE GOOD DIRT

Improving soil health for more
successful gardening

Xanthe White

RANDOM HOUSE
NEW ZEALAND

RANDOM HOUSE

UK | USA | Canada | Ireland | Australia
India | New Zealand | South Africa | China

Random House is an imprint of the Penguin Random House
group of companies, whose addresses can be found at
global.penguinrandomhouse.com.

Penguin
Random House
New Zealand

First published by Penguin Random House
New Zealand, 2016

10 9 8 7 6 5 4 3 2 1

Cover and text design by Carla Sy © Penguin Random
House New Zealand
Front cover photograph by Gavin McWilliam, back cover
photographs by Jessie Casson
Prepress by Image Centre Group
Printed and bound in China by Leo Paper Products Ltd

Image opposite: Hibiscus, nikau and maples mix with
Heliconia, *Salvia* and *Alstroemeria*; a rainbow of colour
illustrates the health of the soil beneath.
Image on page 4: Water rill at Daltons Plantation, Matamata

A catalogue record for this book is available from the
National Library of New Zealand.

ISBN 978-1-77553-854-7

penguin.co.nz

CONTENTS

INTRODUCTION

I'VE HAD A LONG LOVE AFFAIR with dirt. The sort that girls from other parts of the world might not have been allowed. It's dirt, not germs, my father taught me.

We walked barefoot in the mud as children, slipped and slid in it, got covered head to toe in it. I'm not sure you could ever have called me a tomboy; I was dressed in florals and pink and truly believed that one day I would be a princess ballerina. But no one ever told me that mud was not for princesses. Instead we made royal pies from mud and served them at our tea parties.

The earth to me was my grandmother in her green trousers and wellington boots mounding up the potatoes to be ready for Christmas. It was tramps in the mountains and forests where we kept walking in the rain, when we slipped and slid and ached with cold. We were adventurers; this was a sophisticated thing to be. It wasn't until I arrived at my all-girls Catholic secondary school that I started to wonder if maybe this was not the normal approach to life. Somehow my school uniform never looked quite like the others'. There was always something on it, often paint stains acquired in the art room, but always something. The other girls were never as dirty and their ribbons somehow managed to stay in their hair while mine slipped over my face. Still now when I get home my husband knows when I've been drawing because the edges of my arms and hands have ink stuck to the skin.

A good lunch was not around a formal table, it was somewhere lying on the ground with a pile of sandwiches, be it at Nanny's in the Hawke's Bay or our own home. Normally we'd throw a blanket down, but your nose would normally hang over the edge looking at the imperfect lawn with its perfect daisies and the ants dancing busily, hoping for our crumbs when we were done. Down there with your nose on the ground there is a sweet smell like nothing else. A slightly wet smell like rain, slightly sugary like nectar, but just really quite distinctly earthy.

My husband always says we are all stardust thrown into orbit together. I say life is a magical force bubbling on the surface of this earth, transforming from mud to peacock feathers and from saltwater to whale song. If you take all the colours of the rainbow and swirl them together you get the colour of earth. From out of the earth we grow our food, our flowers, green carpets. All the colours re-emerge in moments until they return back into the surface.

In the very thin crust of soil that sits upon the surface of our planet, all the ingredients for the colour of our world are stirred together in various formulas.

We spend little time beneath the earth's surface. After all, through all mythology and teachings, we know that here is where we return to when all is done in this world. And whether you believe in the mother ship or in gods scheming beneath, most of us live where the colours separate beneath the light of the sun.

If you think of earth in this way you can begin to understand how a garden truly works and grows. In the very thin crust of soil that sits upon the surface of our planet, all the ingredients for the colour of our world are stirred together in various formulas. These combinations create different recipes above, which can change the potential beneath the ground. This applies to how nutrient-rich our soil is for both ourselves and the plants we wish to grow. When we learn how to make compost we are taught to add browns and greens, but we should imagine that we are adding the rainbow – packing it down, fluffing it with air, dampening it with rain and returning it to our gardens so the seed we plant can grow again in abundance.

In poorer soils we can still grow, but we are limited to plants that have adapted to these environments. These plants often have smaller leaves hardened to preserve scarce water or hang tight to the ground to save energy. If we wish to grow more, then first we must grow the soil itself. This is a process which takes time and patience, but not a lifetime; and once established the soil becomes self-producing.

I wanted to write this book because I believe the earth beneath is one of our most precious resources and yet it is treated like dirt. Something to be washed away, flattened and scraped bare. Yet this dirt is the source of our wellbeing.

I wanted to write this book because I believe the earth beneath is one of our most precious resources and yet it is treated like dirt. Something to be washed away, flattened and scraped bare. Yet this dirt is the source of our wellbeing. History has taught us that when we lose our soil, our civilisation will follow. In times of plentiful resources we can sustain systems with irrigation and fertilisers, but these methods are imperfect. In time they lead to salination issues and a greater dependence on water. Excesses of nutrients applied to land run the risk of leaching and polluting waterways. And yet the art of good soil is as ancient as great civilisations. We must preserve and maintain our fertile ground, as replacing good soil takes decades. But as gardeners we can also learn to grow living earth that is self-sustaining. The secrets are simple and lie in the waste around us.

I've looked at soil from particle size because for most gardeners this is where the challenges lie. The smaller the particles – such as clay – the harder it is for water to move through, while the larger particles, such as sand and gravel, disperse water quickly and lack organic content. Our aim as gardeners is to either work with our soils and understand their limitations, or to modify them to create living soils suitable for food production.

To understand your own soil you are best to take the time to read this whole book as there are ideas throughout which will be common to all gardeners. The most important thing is to come away with an understanding that good dirt is alive and will grow of its own accord. The recipe for this living earth does not change depending on whether it's on a continent or an island; it is part of the circle of life, carbon from above returned beneath us. The form of that organic matter may change depending on your locality, and the role of water in your landscape will also greatly limit or expand the way you garden, but the principle is the same: return that which was living into the earth so it can live again.

Clay
soils

This ancient forest soil is full of the minerals that were unlocked as the age-old lands were lifted from the sea in underwater volcanic eruptions. For many millions of years the forests upon them developed and stood untouched until the arrival of man some 1,300 years ago. With his initial colonisation of these ancient lands, the first of these forests were cleared to make way for villages and horticulture.

IT WAS NOT UNTIL the intensive agricultural settlements of
Europeans in New Zealand in the 1840s that much of these ancient
forests were cleared by fire and saw at the hand of man, and
transformed into the pasture that now supports dairy and other
agriculture. While in many areas the topsoil is still a remnant, it is
a fragile shell and beneath much of this is heavy clay. The topsoil,
especially on slopes, is easily eroded to reveal a subsoil of clay
which, left exposed to the elements, will harden quickly in the
sun and become impenetrable. But despite its challenges, clay is
a soil that can be brought to life if nurtured and fed.

Clay is the oldest soil in New Zealand, and the finest in
particle size. Soil is defined by its particle size, with clay being one-
thousandth of a speck of sand. If you imagine all soil starts as a rock
– whether it was formed from a volcanic eruption or sedimentation –
and is broken down over time, clay represents a point in the cycle
where the particles become so small that they are close to reforming
to rock in the right conditions. Of course not all soil particles have
followed the process so directly. Some may have been formed from
ash from fires, shells from the ocean and, most importantly to us as
gardeners, by organic matter returning to the earth.

Simply scraping the topsoil back and stockpiling it to be
returned at a later date is not very effective. In this process the
soil loses its life, becomes compacted and oxidises. Scraping back
topsoil is like scraping back the edge of a rocky shore and then
attempting to replace the features. On a rocky shore, if you look
closely, you can see much of the life buzzing away; crabs scuttling
under rocks, sea snails moving slowly, and limpets and barnacles
clinging to the rocks. It is easy to comprehend that this ecology

cannot be scraped back and returned to what it was before. What we need to understand is that the soil beneath is as alive as this delicate foreshore, and when we scrape it away, disposing of the roots and vegetation above and putting aside a pile of earth, we are being just as disruptive. Wherever possible the topsoil above a clay stratum should not only be left undisturbed but also covered with vegetation, weedy or otherwise, to keep its good health until it is ready to be developed.

The most challenging clay soils I have come across in my work are those on subdivisions where the topsoil has been disturbed and the clay hammered and compacted by the machinery of the construction process. To bring a garden back to life after this is a slow and gentle process, even when the topsoil is returned. Because of this, it is advisable, wherever possible, to shift or move the existing topsoil as little as possible if clay is beneath. Of course there are circumstances when adjusting the topography of the land is advantageous, but it should come with an awareness of how the soil will need to be rebuilt.

Clay is a rich soil filled with ancient reserves of minerals and nutrients. The secret to a good clay soil is to unlock these reserves and improve the movement of water through the ground. Clays are dry in summer, especially when left exposed, and they harden and crack like a desert; yet in winter they quickly saturate and become soggy and squishy like a sponge. Digging in wet clay is like kneading bread dough with too much water – it sticks to the spade and to your feet. All gardeners who have experienced a heavy, wet clay are likely to have lost a gumboot that has sunk into the ground and stayed there as they attempted to step forward.

These qualities of being so malleable when wet and yet so hard when fired beneath the heat of the sun are what has made clay soils ideal for pottery and ceramics.

This is the soil of my childhood; burnt orange clay that my grandmother, who lived in Taranaki where the fertile soil is abundant, cursed as she helped my father dig his vegetable beds. Now, though, my father's garden has more than a foot of high-quality topsoil in its beds. Years of composting our family's waste and adding bags of compost has seen the living soil build and grow. Decades of returning organic matter into the land has completely restored the soil to a healthy and productive loam. This is the best approach to a clay soil, I believe: to build your topsoil slowly layer upon layer over time. Compost and mulch, compost and mulch, season after season. This is a practice that happens naturally as we garden.

My mother-in-law and her husband own a seven-acre block of Waikato clay. They planted their orchard on a beautifully positioned north-facing bank. The aspect was ideal, but over the years the desirable sun had hardened the heavy clay paddocks to rock, and planting a tree required a pickaxe and hard labour. While the fruit trees slowly and steadily managed to push their roots into the soil, the bank itself grew little more than globe artichokes. No one complained of the abundant fields of beautiful flowers, or the fresh artichoke served with Nana's homemade hollandaise, or the good fruit, but this prime spot was not fulfilling its potential. Then came the kunekune pigs Francis Bacon and George Orwell, who took over the bank with a vengeance. The windfall apples and pears belonged to them. They greeted the kitchen scraps with pleasure, and gave us enthusiastic deep groans as we rubbed behind their hairy ears. They were happy as pigs in muck, and as winter came on the field became a trampled brown mud bath. The grassy meadow was never the same again. Looking over the neighbours' elegantly formalised garden was a field of muck.

Various tricks and treats were attempted to rein in the rooting pigs, but eventually the decision was made that it was time for them to retire to another block in Raglan. Or so the story goes. But what was left was a wonderfully improved soil. The kitchen scraps had been efficiently processed by the pigs, and the fruit trees had been doing their own work, dropping fruit and leaf each season. Now paths weave through the trees and are dreamily planted with herbs and pollinators, berries and daffodil bulbs, and the artichokes still seed through the plantings each year. At the bottom of the hill a beehive has arrived, too, and what was once a laborious paddock is now an abundant and beautiful forest of food.

The wonderful thing with a garden is that the process of creating soil is not something we gardeners fight against – our gardens are on our side, working alongside us. The more we plant, the more the life of the garden perpetuates, and as long as organic matter is returned into the soil, the soil will grow and the plants' health will continue to prosper.

SOIL APPROACH

WHEN TEACHING PEOPLE TO PLANT in clay soils, reminding them that most of the pots we garden in are formed from clay can help to explain what *not* to do. A clean-cut hole in a clay soil filled with good-quality mix is akin to creating a pot beneath the surface. In winter, when water is plentiful, the hole is prone to fill with water which enjoys this vacuum, and, if no allowance has been made to help the water drain away, many plants' roots will drown or become stressed. This is because, while most plants love water, there is a difference between sitting water and moving water.

A soil where the water is not moving is quickly identified by the smell. This should not be mistaken for the rich and heady aroma of a healthy compost, which, while it can be quite rich to the nose, is distinct from an anaerobic soil lacking in oxygen. The best description I can use is that it's as if you have dug up some old socks – a dusty, putrid smell. Another sign of a lack of water movement in a clay soil is a greyness in colour. This environment is the same to plants as an airless room is to us. Stale air and stale earth both lack oxygen, which is as important to life beneath the surface as it is to life above.

DESIGNING A PLANTING HOLE

SO, WHILE A CLEANLY CUT HOLE can create more trouble than it's worth, the best results are from a rough and jagged hole with some high-value organic mass at the base – such as sheep pellets – and a generous dose of gypsum to help the distribution of water. A rough base of clay creates lots of crevices that a plant's roots can push into to unlock the minerals and create tunnels into the soil beneath. The organic matter attracts microbial life and beneficial fungi that live symbiotically (with both benefiting) alongside a plant's roots.

One of the best ways to ensure water can be directed into and away from a plant's roots is to create holes on a slope. Channels in the holes create underground waterways that can – when dug leading into the hole at the top of the slope – direct water into the base of a tree or – when the channel faces downwards from the slope – ensure excess water has an escape route. Often a combination can be most effective, i.e. a single channel at the top of the hill and to a 35° angle from the most downward point. This encourages water to enter quickly, but then slow down and gently trickle out.

Another method of ensuring that a plant's roots do not become waterlogged is to dig a vase-shaped hole and plant in a soft mound within the hole. Mounding is a common technique in gardening, but it needs to be done correctly. The slope of the mound does not need to be very great – 30° maximum but as soft as 15° will help to lift the shallow roots above the surface when the ground is waterlogged. The vase shape beneath overflows more easily than a deep square hole. It is most important that the height of the soil sits correctly around a plant's roots. Different plants have different levels of tolerance to soil, either removed from their root systems or loaded against their stems, but generally it is not a good idea to heavily raise the level of soil around a plant's trunk or stem. Changes in soil level on the surface can also suffocate a plant's roots that sit on the surface.

When thinking about life below the surface you should also understand that there are different parts of a root system that have different roles. For example, a tree's roots that sit on the surface are different from those that grow very deep below, and can be quite sensitive to being driven on or covered over with heavy soils. This should not be confused with a mulch, which is simply mimicking a natural cycle of debris that is continuously being littered on the soil in a healthy garden.

CHINA'S HILLS OF POTS

IN THE LOESS PLATEAU IN CHINA efforts to reclaim the landscape have been taken to a new level. Soils have become so depleted in this region that the line of the desert has begun moving forward, devouring any remnants of life. Initial efforts to plant trees were unsuccessful, with high proportions dying. Now, however, 1,000 acres of hillsides have been planted with date trees, and each tree has its own clay-like terrace hand-crafted around it to ensure that water and organic matter are captured as the trees require. This highly labour-intensive method is still the most productive way to reclaim land that would otherwise turn to dust.

GREEN MULCHES

GREEN MULCH IS AN ESSENTIAL ELEMENT to a clay soil, and helps to create a verdant garden. It can be temporary, such as mustard sown over fallow paddocks or vegetable beds, which allows a soil to return to fertility; or permanent, such as creeping plants like *Leptinella spp* and *Selliera spp* that cover the soil and keep the ground beneath cool and fertile.

Green mulches are an effective way of growing a living soil in clay. Plants such as lupins and comfrey have deep roots that are very efficient at moving through such a soil, mining the nutrients and pulling them to the surface as they grow. These plants can then be harvested for compost or teas that can be used to dress a garden; or they can simply be laid as a mulch over vegetable beds. Not only do these deep roots mean the leaves are rich in otherwise inaccessible goodness, they also create pathways through the soil and allow water, fungi and microbes to move freely through the earth beneath.

It should be understood, though, that plants like comfrey and lupin are vigorous plants and are thus difficult to remove. As with all gardening, we need to understand the differences in our local environment and make careful choices that are appropriate to each particular site. In the South Island, wilding lupins are beautiful but problematic as there is little to out-compete them. Comfrey has such deep roots that, once in place, only the most determined will be able to get rid of it. Out in an orchard comfrey can be an appropriate choice, but planted in a small vegetable garden it will have you tearing your hair out as the comfrey out-competes your beans and tomatoes.

In situations where the topsoil has been removed back to deeper levels of the strata and a site has been hardened by construction, the soil needs to be restored with care. In my experience the best approach is to attempt to recreate some strata. In my early years of landscaping I was faced with many sites like this, and I attempted to fill new garden beds with the finest of planting mixes. What I found from these experiences is that a high-quality mix and a clay soil are like oil and water. Rather than binding, the good soil sits above and the clay beneath. The plants' roots tend to stay in the soft soil above and sulk as they hit the heavier clay. By using an intermediate layer of topsoil between the clay and planting mix, the soil structure in terms of water flow and root systems is far superior. A good layer of gypsum between the topsoil and the clay also helps to bind the layers, as it improves the flow of water from one layer to the next. Sometimes in gardening you can have too much of a good thing.

In these circumstances mulching is of absolute importance. This not only adds substance and body to the soil as it breaks down, but in the layers between the soil and the mulch all sorts of life exists.

When we mulch we mimic leaf litter, and in leaf litter there is abundant life at work. In the same way as microbial life in our bodies is essential to our wellbeing it is essential to the earth. The insects, bacteria and fungi work in communities to create a healthy living soil that is ideal for gardening. The root systems depend on this activity for the transference of nutrients, water and protection from soil-borne pathogens.

MATERIALS

THE MATERIALS THAT ARE MOST USEFUL in a clay soil are those that will improve water flow and the development of topsoil. Good drainage is key, and so seeking materials that are porous is desirable. While we want water to be able to move through the soil beneath the surface, it is also difficult to retain water when it is scarce, as the fine soil particles harden and water flows over the top, failing to reach the roots below. This is improved by the use of mulches and composts that encourage topsoil to build on the surface. With clay the process is slow and steady. Layer upon layer over time will create a soil that, once established, will maintain its growth without our efforts, but a gardener must show patience.

Terracotta and broken crockery

Most gardeners are very familiar with terracotta pots. In container gardening they are ideal for keeping plant roots at the perfect temperature, and they have a degree of permeability that stops saturation without rotting, like wood. The use of terracotta in growing media is an expensive technique used commonly in hydroponic systems, but also to grow specialty plants that like free-draining soil. While expensive, it is a very stable way of creating aeration and drainage. Planting a garden this way, though, is not practical or sustainable – unless you are at a Greek wedding! Thankfully most of us don't break enough crockery on a daily basis to supply all our gardening needs. Broken crockery and plant pots in compost and in planting holes is well worth utilising, though. Smashing the pots up to the size of one-dollar coins or smaller is ideal.

Gypsum

Gypsum is a form of calcium which occurs in natural deposits. It is essentially the same as the chalk we used on our blackboards at school and in plasterboards used for internal walls.

When you were a child you may have put chalk in food colouring and watched how the water was drawn up into the chalk. It is this quality that makes gypsum so valuable in the conditioning of soils, particularly clay soils. Gypsum comes in the form of a fine dust, and care should be taken not to breathe it in, as small particles are not desirable in our lungs.

Scoria and pumice

Like biochar (see page 122) and terracotta, scoria and pumice create aeration in soil. Scoria and pumice are both formed through the volcanic process where the magma or lava cools so quickly that the gases which mixed through the magna and ash are captured as the rock cools, leaving holes throughout the structure of the stone. This is wonderful for growth. Above ground, if it is kept wet, pumice or scoria will first grow moss, which is like a hydroponic carpet upon which other plants can then grow. Beneath the earth, pumice and scoria not only assist the flow of water through a landscape, they are occupied by essential fungi and microorganisms that create a growing soil.

Sheep pellets, sheep dags and cow patties

In New Zealand sheep pellets have long been one of the most beneficial soil conditioners and are available in plentiful quantities. However, the manure mixed with sheep dags straight from the woolshed is even better, if you can get your hands on it. The sheep dag is the wool cut from the sheep's bottom that is clotted with faeces. The combination of the wool fibre and the manure is all a soil needs. There was a time when you were paid to clean these up, but now this by-product of the wool and lamb industry is highly valued as a commodity in its own right. Cow patty fertiliser is not as readily available but, given the number of cows out there producing it, it's about time someone made it available as a soil conditioner in its own right.

WORMS

MOST OF US GROW UP KNOWING that worms are good for the earth, but less common knowledge is that in New Zealand there are over 171 native species of worm and 23 introduced species. The common earthworm, which was the focus of the last work published by Charles Darwin, is a foreigner to our soils, and is the only worm in New Zealand which brings its casting to the surface, adding fertility to the soil.

Our native worms are deeper dwellers and are only found in association with native plants. While the castings of these worms may not build topsoil in the way that the lumbricid worms Darwin observed in his own garden in Kent did, their relationship with the quality of soil is of equal importance within their unique ecology. The largest of our earthworms is over a metre in length and lives deep beneath the surface. This offers some explanation as to the length of kiwis' beaks: the reward of a metre-long worm is worth growing such a tool for.

Whichever part of the soil strata these worms are working in, their task is the same – they both aerate and move rich organic matter through the strata, which is essential for the health of plants. Worms are like the farmers of the world beneath, and are exactly what a clay soil calls for – moving through the soil, spreading microbes which are essential to all life, and creating tunnels of air that make for a healthy flow of both water and oxygen. This is exactly what clays can lack: permeability.

It would be reasonable to assume that the relationship between worms and the plants above is one of symbiosis; when a forest is cleared, the earthworms which live deep below the surface disappear at the same rate. How important worms are to soil health can be measured in actual weight: the number of worms beneath the surface in a healthy forest is actually greater than the mass of all the creatures above.

For food production, the introduced earthworms are the most efficient. While they were probably introduced to New Zealand accidentally in the soil and leaf matter of plants that were brought from around the world, they have thrived in the altered landscape. They do, however, disperse completely from a pasture when native forests return, and are replaced by our native species as birds are above. The reason earthworms are so desired in agriculture is that they can produce up to 1 centimetre of topsoil in a year. This may not sound like much, but in terms of productivity it is gardener's gold.

COVER UP

CULTIVATING THE GROUND ALSO GREATLY REDUCES the number of earthworms below. The efficiencies of machines ploughing fields should be measured against the loss of earthworms and the amount of topsoil production you will be losing. Like

everything, there are times when this may be called for, but the least disturbance makes for less work in the long term.

As well as reducing worms, beneficial fungus and microbial life in the soil, leaving earth exposed to the sun oxidises it. You can put the very best soil onto a garden but you will lose some of its value if you leave it bare. Leaving soil exposed also increases the rate of water loss significantly. In hot countries such as the United Arab Emirates, plants are planted shoulder to shoulder; this is because the best way to preserve water loss in extreme circumstances is to ensure that the land is covered in growth. Nothing cools the earth or reduces water loss with the same efficiency as plant life.

PLANTING

CLAY SOILS ARE FOREST SOILS. In mature forests, much of the biomass is above ground. Plants live not just on the forest floor, where competition for nutrients is intense, but off the living wood of other plants and trees. Where forest has been cleared, what topsoil there is can be unstable. Unfortunately, most forests have been cleared by slash-and-burn methods, with not much of the biomass being returned to the soil. Biomass can be returned by composting, adding biochar, hugelkultur (see page 132) or a combination of methods.

Plants that do well in clay soils are those with strong root networks that are able to push through the otherwise compacted soil to create an aerated earth suitable for healthy growth. The plants best adapted to these zones are native species that have been competing in these forest soils for centuries. Normally in a forest

it is when a giant tree falls that the opportunity for reoccupying a space becomes available. In these situations the competition is hot and there are many plants that sit on the forest floor ready to make a race for the top when the starter gun fires and the light reaches the ground. Any plant that is not adapted to the local soils is at a disadvantage. While we may bemoan a clay soil compared to the volcanic ash or loam of a neighbour, across the planet many plants have adapted to survive in conditions far worse, and they find our soils abundant in comparison. This is why we must take great care when planting exotics. There are many plants that can provide us with food and flowers

> Exotic plants may have a high value for medicine, honeybees or herbs. These values are part of what connects us to the land and should not be dismissed too readily.

that will not pervade beyond the boundaries of our gardens. While these exotic plants may not conserve the amazing plant life that is unique to New Zealand, they may have a high value with regard to medicine, honeybees or herbs. These values are part of what connects us to the land and should not be dismissed too readily, but we must ensure that we do not do great harm either when we garden. It is a fine dance done best by taking heed of the experience of others who have experimented before us. Valuable lessons have been learnt in the past.

ECOLOGICAL BANDS

CLAY SOILS THAT HAVE BEEN CLEARED of forest and have suffered erosion may need to be put to rest where their productivity is low. Native plants are ideal for re-establishing a landscape where farming may have been deemed inappropriate. They are adapted to the soil, so no modification is required. If close to a bush reserve, a few key species that attract bird life and stabilise soil will see diversity develop naturally over time, as these birds bring seeds to the soil. There is much benefit to us in having stable lands that can protect productive land and maintain the quality of air and water.

Revegetation of native forests or wetlands, coasts or hillsides is one of the most interesting areas of landscape design that places New Zealand in a different realm to the rest of the world. The process of reforestation using nursery plants such as manuka and flaxes as a catalyst is well developed in New Zealand. In low-yield areas on farms, such as hillsides, manuka and phormium (flax) are among the species that can also create income in the form of honey.

When reforesting or planting your land you should still take time to consider the design of the landscape and the different zones, or bands, that you are looking for. If it is land that you are to live on, look at combinations of natives to create wind shelter; or combinations that will remain competitive but low-growing so that views are retained, versus areas where you would like full forest. You may have water run-off and be looking for plants that are excellent for water filtration. In each of these categories you should work with a medley of between 15 and 25 species. Diversification makes for healthier plantings and has a better strike rate, whatever your soil. These should be planted in a random mosaic to create a natural feel. When you have multiple zones you will have crossover species that are useful in different areas, such as flax. This helps with continuity and connections between the different landscapes. Aspect may also affect your planting zones. Your soil will benefit greatly from these mixed plantings. Think of the Indian farmer who plants his mixture of crops on the fields before he plants his main crop. This is to get balance into the soil, which is just as important in native plantings as it is in a food garden.

THERE IS NO DOUBT that there is a difference in the productivity of a clay soil depending on your average rainfall. While a squelchy clay soil has its problems, it is much easier to modify than a hardened clay. As water above ground is the source of all life, the way water moves through soil is just as critical. Where there is abundant water, large-leafed plants will make good use of the excess, and a clay soil with a healthy topsoil is like a sponge. When the soil is dry, though, it contracts and splits apart, making it hard to get much-needed organic matter into the ground. This is where cover is essential, both canopy and ground cover.

If there was one garden to teach us how to pull the fruits of a garden from a clay earth paddock, it would have to be Bev McConnell's Ayrlies Garden in southeast Auckland. There is no other with which to compare. What defines it, I believe, is that it is formed very much from the eye of the artist, not the engineer. It is not so much an imprint on the land but a life's work and an example of what can be achieved when you allow a garden to take you on a journey, not just through the landscape, but through the seasons and the years.

Water, too, follows the lay of the land, and this manipulation is one of the successes of Ayrlies Garden. There is barely a level path to be seen. Instead, the garden rolls and undulates into the natural lay of the land. It has not become so without the help of diggers and heavy machinery, but there is a sensitivity to the landscape that considers how water flows through the soil beneath as much

as the soil above. Bev McConnell's garden was inspired by her contemporary Beth Chatto, who now at the age of ninety is still a mentor to many designers. What she taught Bev about the garden was that you do not need a manor house to have a beautiful garden; you just need to learn to understand your land – where it is wet and where it is dry, as well as how the heat of the sun and prevailing winds have both shaped and will continue to shape the land.

This sort of thinking teaches us to map our landscapes before we alter them in any way, and helps us understand the importance of the contour of a garden in creating different environments above the ground. To simply retain and flatten is a somewhat crude approach to a garden. Its advantages are obvious when a game of tennis needs to be played, or even cricket perhaps, but it is often taken beyond a productive function to serve only as a reminder of where the imagination has ended.

WATER IN CLAY

IF YOU ARE HAVING TROUBLE IMAGINING where water might flow beneath the ground, think first of its patterns above: they are likely to follow a similar path. There is nothing more unsettling than a water feature that defies gravity or common sense. Words of wisdom came to Witi Ihimaera from his grandmother when he came home from his first day at school and recited the nursery rhyme *Jack and Jill*. 'What are these Pakeha teaching you, boy? Everyone knows you don't head uphill to look for water!' Water, like most of us, follows the path of least resistance. First you should understand the original source of your water and where it is headed. It is normally on its way to the sea, or to join a larger river or stream, perhaps passing through a lake. Underneath it is no different – water follows aqueducts beneath the surface and seeps slowly from

rain or snowfall heading to a larger source. Some water is very
obvious in winter months where the earth becomes soft and spongy,
or ponds and streams appear in areas otherwise dry. But you can
be sure that where the water flows in the wet season is the path it
follows in summer months, too, even it beneath the surface.

While creating a garden that follows these patterns there is
sometimes cause to shift water out of areas such as a house site and
the areas that surround it. If you direct this water into the natural
paths, a feature can be made of it both above and below.

If we follow a curve on the landscape rather than interrupting
it, if our paths wind through and across these contours, the results
are a delight, and Ayrlies Garden is a living example of that.

The position of gardens in terms of the water will determine
the appropriate style of the garden. Dry and arid plants suited to
a Mediterranean or alpine garden can be grown in clay soils, but
only those that are exposed and facing the sun at the top of a hill,
not those that become sodden in winter months. It is not enough
to just classify the soil particles and ignore the patterns of water.
Nature is never that simple.

NATURE AND HYDROPONICS

IN SINGAPORE, THE SOILS ARE LONG stripped of topsoil, and
even in planters the soil that is often used is a clay. Rainfall and
warmth are plentiful and the clay soils seem to be used to cool
the plants in the heat. The amount of water ensures they do not
dry and harden, and so the level of organic matter seems less
important. Where water is plentiful, access to nutrients is easy for
the large leafy plants that prosper in this climate, demonstrating
how much the structure of the soil's relationship to water affects
the gardens we create. In the tropics, soils are relatively poor,

yet plants flourish as the high rainfall moves nutrients through a deeply layered jungle of green matter. Take a close look at any tropical leaf and see how the leaves are designed to collect and pass water over the plant's roots. Hold a hose on a banana leaf, a ligularia leaf or a puka leaf, and watch how these large pans collect and direct water to the stem and then to the roots, collecting any organic matter such as bird droppings, soil, bark or humus along the way. Soil in forests does not need to be rich as the biomass is held and cycled above the ground with surprising efficiency because of the high rainfall. High rainfall means that nutrients move quickly through a system, and so if the forest above is removed the quality of the soil is quickly eroded.

> Hold a hose on a banana leaf, a ligularia leaf or a puka leaf, and watch how these large pans collect and direct water to the stem and then to the roots, collecting any organic matter such as bird droppings, soil, bark or humus along the way.

COVERED EARTH

JAPAN HAS SOILS VERY SIMILAR to New Zealand, and clay is common. Both groups of islands have crept from the sea as tectonic plates rise and fall. This brittle edge of the Earth's crust chooses its moments to remind both nations that its work continues at depths we can only imagine. But it is also the source of the minerals that have fed the surface from beneath over millions of years.

Japanese gardeners have had many thousands of years to consider how the clay earth can be cultivated. You will never see earth left bare in a Japanese garden, unless it is a track upon which you are to walk. Where an unpaved flat plane or open space is required, groundcovers or mosses are used to cool the earth beneath. What surprised me most while working in Japan was the variation between my idea of soil and the Japanese idea. Japanese gardens have been formed for centuries, long before modern composting and production methods were widely practised as they are in New Zealand. The beautiful earth that we take for granted is hard to get in many other countries. Yet in Japan they have managed to use clay to their advantage. The traditional Japanese gardens are expressions of nature, and the earth within them is moulded to contours that disguise the hand of man. In one project I was working with my contractor's father, who was a highly respected landscape architect well into his eighties. He was a tiny man and had come to work with me from his hospital bed as we placed a very special rock 3 metres high into the garden. He sat in a wheelchair with a face mask on and his walking stick at his side, his ankles swollen with his condition, and orchestrated the team as the rock was pulled into position. Around the rock we had to mound the earth to create hills. As he spoke little English, we exchanged ideas in sketches back and forth on how we saw this landscape to be. We agreed on much, but when it came to the mound he wanted steep inclines, while I argued they should be softer, more rolling. It wasn't until that evening when I was eating my dinner and looking across to the hills beyond that I saw how in our heads we had two different

OPPOSITE ABOVE
Japanese designer
Yosuke Yamaguchi follows
traditional design methods,
adopting natural forms
that allow for the free flow
of water.

OPPOSITE BELOW
Traditional paths have
minimal impact on the
ground surface, allowing the
soil to breathe and grow.

versions of nature. My head was full of the hills of the Waikato, rolling like pregnant curves, while he was dreaming of the hills around Nagasaki that plunge into the sea like jagged rocks on the shore.

MOSS

MOSS IS VERY VALUABLE TO CLAY soils and plays an interesting role in natural systems. In fact it is on this role that French botanist Patrick Blanc's great vertical gardens have been based. Blanc has studied how moss acts as a spongy and mineral-rich mat that allows other plants to grow in precarious positions. The cover that moss provides helps to cool the roots beneath and also filters water evenly, creating a penetrable surface that then draws the water down. This is wonderful for a heavy clay soil that, if left uncovered, becomes hard in the summer time and in winter rain suffers very poor permeability, becoming oversaturated.

Moss and fungus are the first to form on old tree trunks fallen to the forest floor. Fungi are absolutely essential to plant systems and the formation and health of a soil. While there are certainly aesthetic drivers in the use of moss in Japanese gardens, it is believed that the gentle way a Japanese garden is managed is how the moss lawns first developed. Most modern gardening encourages as little disruption to the soil as possible. We understand that soil itself grows over time, and that by pushing it around or digging it over we risk disrupting its health. Japanese have long practised this approach, and while they rake and sweep back leaves they do little to disrupt the soil itself. The use of rocks helps support the formation of moss by creating nooks where it will grow. Moss is surprisingly tolerant of sweeping, and in fact flourishes under such treatment.

TERRACING

TERRACES ARE ONE OF THE OLDEST and most effective ways
of managing sloping land to achieve productivity. New Zealand
landscape designer Andy Hamilton has spent the past decade
working in the studio of Tom Stuart Smith, designing projects
across the globe from India to Morocco as well as in the English
countryside. A garden in Somerset is one of his most recent
projects, completed before Hamilton returned to set up his
studio in Auckland in 2015. While walled terraces have been
used for many thousands of years for agricultural purposes, in
a large garden they are labour-intensive and expensive to build.
In this Somerset garden Hamilton has used a cut-and-batter
method (see on page 52). Clay soils with their fine particles and
stability are ideal for a cut-and-batter system, unlike a sand soil,
which would fall away quickly. As the site was prepared, soil
was peeled back in profiles and stored in separate piles so they
were able to reinstate the clay and loam as close to the original
layers as possible. While there are disadvantages to earthworks,
improvement in land management is a good reason to move
earth, and taking care to preserve existing soil types and profiles
lessens the disadvantages.

Water management was also an important aspect of the
Somerset garden. One of the key features of the design was to
capture water from a spring that had created a bog on the lower
area and pump it back to the top so it could be redistributed
through a rill system and feed the garden beds as required. The
even distribution of water in clay soils is of great assistance in

growing soil and preserving existing soil reserves, especially on sloping sites. Hamilton's experience throughout the world has had a huge focus on water management, with gardens in Morocco and India needing careful attention.

CUT AND BATTER

CUT AND BATTER IS WHEN YOU take an even or undulating contour and both cut and fill the ground to create easily manageable level terraces and steeper banks to be planted. It is surprising how steeply you can batter a bank to be planted, resulting in deep layers of planting rather than a hard, unattractive retaining wall. Planting in a garden like this needs little height, and the ideal plants to use are grasses, flaxes, small shrubs and hardy perennials. You should also consider plants that have deep root systems to ensure the batter remains stable. Annuals or vegetables are not as useful on a gradient, as constant disruption of sloping soil will cause erosion over time. You also need to make sure you plant full sweeps and leave no soil bare, as the steeper the gradient the more difficult constant mulching becomes. There are a range of wool cloths which can be used on very steep slopes to help stabilise the soil while plants establish. They are not attractive but are very effective if you are concerned about soil run-off in the short term.

INGREDIENTS GUIDE

GYPSUM

Helps to separate the particles of a clay soil without shifting acidity as lime does. Good to use when planting to assist root development.

DOLOMITE LIME

Helps to separate clay particles and also lowers acidity if needed. Dolomite contains magnesium, which is essential for plant and human health.

SHEEP PELLETS

The combination of wool and manure assists both in the nutrient content and the structure of a soil, activating its organic matter.

COMPOST

Should be spread thinly or mixed through soil at planting. Compost is rich and should be laid in spring and autumn or between plantings.

SCORIA

This porous rock helps to drain water out of oversaturated soils. Ideal for drainage and in planting trees and shrubs.

BARK MULCH

A heavier bark mulch should be used for woodier plants, while a finer mulch should be used for perennials and borders. Take care not to build mulch up around a plant's stem or trunk.

LEAF MULCH

Leaves can be collected and allowed to compost on new beds, or used to create leaf mould to mulch beds in spring and autumn.

TERRACOTTA

Great as a drainage material helping air flow and water movement in heavy soils.

BIOCHAR

Holds nutrients, microbes and moisture in the soil in a very stable state. Effective in creating stable living soil systems and assisting with water aeration in heavy clays.

WOOD

Think of wood like a wick that can pull water out of a saturated soil or hold it in an arid soil. Wood can be buried or laid over the surface.

PLANTING APPROACH

Clay soils need patience. Layer upon layer of food over time will reward you.

Make sure you allow water to move through the soil base. When digging holes make sure they are loose, not clean cut. A smoothly cut hole can harden like pottery, confining both water and a plant's roots.

While bare soil is never ideal, bare clay is a disaster. It hardens in the sun and water slips over the surface. Planting or mulch helps saturation on the surface and reduces soil temperatures.

Mounding plants above the ground helps roots stay out of over-saturated soil. It is important that the mound is soft and covers roots but does not raise the soil level around a plant's stem or trunk.

Digging clay soils is best in autumn and spring when the soil is softened but not saturated. In summer it can be too hard and in winter too squelchy!

If planting a clay bank where mulches are difficult, use a biodegradable erosion cloth, such as coconut fibre or wool-based cloth, to protect the soil as plants establish. Select deep-rooting grasses to help stabilise crumbly ground.

Fertile soils

Fertile soils come in many forms – from blended loams and topsoils remnant of ancient forests or grasslands, to silts laid down from ancient riverbeds, or beautiful volcanic ash thrown from violent eruptions in a distant past. Gardeners who have sought these soils or landed them by accident might think their fingers green, and so they may be, but they should also give homage to the processes that formed them and the enormity of time that it took for these productive depths to grow.

AS GARDENERS WE CAN CONTINUE TO maintain and nurture the ground beneath or we can take it for granted and let it wash to the seas. Many civilisations before us have slowly worked through their soils and, while the word we live in is different and ever-changing, it is upon the soil and water we can most depend when times are hard. We can do without many things, but from the soil comes the sustenance of life and to the soil many of us will be returned.

SOIL APPROACH

FERTILE SOILS ARE OFTEN TAKEN FOR granted. The best advice is to work the soil with as little disruption as possible, and let the worms help the soil continue to grow. Constant tilling and clearing can see good soil lost at an alarmingly fast rate, especially on slopes. Leaving a soil exposed to the sun oxidises it, therefore, if you can keep the earth covered it will retain greater fertility. This fertility comes not just from the nutrient content of the soil but from the bacteria, fungi and insects that form part of a healthy earth. Interestingly, contact with this living system has been shown to increase our own immunity to disease and increase happiness. Why exactly we are still not sure, but I do know the good feelings I get from working with soil, putting my nose to the earth and feeling it through my fingers.

Continuing to mulch a soil from above will ensure that it continues to grow, as well as retain its existing structure. You should also make a conscious effort to measure what you are taking out of a soil in terms of organic matter when you prune and harvest, and then return it to the soil.

When planting, make an effort to disturb the existing structure as little as possible. Make sure that soil levels around a plant's stem are even, but you should not need to mound or manipulate the ground other than making room for the root ball.

SILT

SILT IS A VERY DESIRABLE SOIL. It sits in size between clay and sand, making it more workable than clay but not as unstable as sand. Silts are created when rocks are worn away by water or ice over a long period of time. It is the silts of the river Nile that make this area one of the most sustainably fertile agricultural systems in human history. And it is because of this agricultural history that part of Africa was able to make great advances. Flooding is what shifts the fine particles into the land, and the Nile had an annual flooding cycle, which delivered fresh silt to the riverbanks for many thousands of years. But the fertile soils came at a price, and the inconsistency in the volume or path of the floods meant that some years the floods would wipe out crops and other years they would fall short. This natural system was altered with the building of the Aswan Dam between 1898 and 1902. This has allowed control over water for crops, which reduces the unpredictability of the flooding. The price of this, though, is that those valuable silts that fed the arid plains of Egypt through many great civilisations now build up behind the dam. While Egypt is no longer faced with the unpredictability of Mother Nature, the impact on the soils in the region has been notable. Whether it is because of the lack of silt content or because of irrigation, salination is an increasing problem in this region. Salt is the last thing you want in your soil, as in high enough doses it is as toxic to plants as it can be to us.

For all the variations within the soil the most important is particle size, as this affects how freely both water and nutrients as well as fungi and bacteria can move and live within it. Clay soils are so ancient and fine that there is little space between the particles, making it hard for water and plant roots as well as other life to permeate. Sandy soils are too permeable and unstable, with water dispersing quickly beyond the root zones of the plants. The structure of the soil is very fluid, and it is harder for roots to grip onto and for organic material to form a good topsoil above. Silt sits in particle size between these two and retains water evenly, which helps in the processing of organic matter. This makes silt the ideal soil for growing.

> It is the silts of the river Nile that make this area one of the most sustainably fertile agricultural systems in human history. And it is because of this agricultural history that part of Africa was able to make great advances.

VOLCANIC EARTH

MY OWN GARDEN SITS on a 2-metre-deep bed of volcanic ash that fell over 50,000 years ago. The maunga that sits beside us was formed when the lava beneath exploded to the surface. It flowed upwards, filling the 500-metre crater the explosion had created, and overflowed to form three large hills and a lava trail 10 kilometres long, until it reached the sea and cooled. In the mountain behind our house there are lava caves winding beneath the ground, some discovered and some hidden. In our own back yard, miniature tunnels reveal themselves from time to time when we dig beneath. This extraordinary process that has formed the Auckland landscape is somewhat terrifying if considered too closely. The cold comfort of living on the crater's edge of such a violent explosion is that Auckland's volcanoes have to date only exploded once in each location.

The gift from this precarious landscape, however, is the soil that results from such a violent act of nature. The lava, which is the heart of our planet, is essentially a flow of molten stardust carrying an ideal mineral composition for starting life. Rangitoto Island is Auckland's only volcano that is known to have erupted multiple times, most recently just 550 to 600 years ago. From it we can observe the slow process as life returns to the field of scoria boulders that litter much of the surface. It builds back slowly as seabirds and winds bring matter onto the craggy surface. The ocean, too, throws up seaweed and flotsam and jetsam. As the first seeds of hardy plants such as manuka or hebe take root into the fertile surface, they begin the process of restoring organic matter to the earth. Every leaf that drops and branch that falls is a store of energy for the further regeneration of the landscape.

Volcanic soils have their challenges, especially if you are located close to a lava flow, and the topsoil can be pulled back to reveal a solid form of what was once liquid rock. Where this happens, the only way to plant is up, unless you want to bring in some heavy machinery to mine the earth. Plants can still thrive, though, in the soils above. And while trees sometimes struggle to find a way beneath with their roots, most gardens close to maunga are abundant. Auckland's lava also forms caves that wind beneath the ground. While most gardeners won't be faced with such curiosities, entering these caves is a wonderful way to get a sense of the cool environment most plants inhabit in the earth beneath.

TOPSOIL AND LOAM

LOAM IS THE TERM GIVEN TO a soil that is essentially a mix of the various soil types with a decent amount of organic content. You can have a clay loam, sandy loam or a silty loam – they are named by the soil type that's present in the largest quantity. Most topsoils are loams, and these, whatever their basis, are the most desirable soils for horticulturalists and gardeners, and are wonderful for growing in. The term can also refer to an artificial mix, and you can create a loam soil on a clay, sand, silt or gravel base by adding organic matter over time. While they are the easiest soils to grow in and to build greater soil reserves on, loams can easily be lost by poor management, leaving the land stripped back.

> Most topsoils are loams, and these, whatever their basis, are the most desirable soils for horticulturalists and gardeners, and are wonderful for growing in.

The loss of topsoil happens fastest off hillsides and sloping land that is cleared and run with stock. The bigger the animals, the faster the erosion of topsoil because of the disruption of the surface. Deer, for example, are well known to cause fast erosion of soils. The most effective way to intensively farm sloping land is to terrace, which allows for the capturing of water and organic matter. This has been practised in Asia with rice terraces and in many other parts of the world with relative success for centuries, as long as it has been used alongside active composting and there is sufficient rainfall or water reserves to support growth. Other productive systems that work on steeper land are forest systems – for timber or food production. Food forest systems are based on the traditional managed forest systems of the Amazonians.

GOOD SOIL

SOIL VARIES GREATLY IN COLOUR and texture; and, while a
blacker soil is often a sign of richness, fertile soils come in many
colours. So, apart from performance, how can you tell which soils
are likely to perform and which will create challenges? Particle
size is the best general indicator that the soil is going to be good
for growing. Each morning I mulch my potted orange tree with
the leftover grinds from my stovetop espresso, partly because
it's the closest plant pot to the kitchen, but also because the tree's
hungry roots mean I'm constantly refreshing the soil in its pot.
With some worm juice added, this provides some of the nutrient
that you need to keep a citrus productive. The coffee grinds are
about the perfect consistency for an ideal soil – not gritty like
a sand or sticky like a clay. Another way to tell a fertile soil is to
squeeze a clump of damp soil together in your hand. A clay soil
will stick together in a tight ball, holding its form even if shaken;
a sandy soil will fall away as soon as you open your hand; but the
fertile soil sits between these. It will clump together loosely, and
then be easily shaken apart again.

PRESERVING SOILS

WHILE SILT IS VERY DESIRABLE in a natural soil, it is less than
ideal in water systems. As fertiliser run-off causes problems
in waterways, so do increased silts, which are a result of land
erosion. Planting along waterways is not just advantageous for
creating clean waterways, it also slows the loss of topsoil and
nutrients from the land itself. While we still have large reserves of
desirable loam in New Zealand, there are signs in the landscape
of this slipping away in steep areas that have been cleared for

pasture. This is worth some consideration, because if we compare the soils we have and the timeframes involved in their formation, it is not a resource we want to have to wait to reform. Twenty centimetres of topsoil takes a very healthy field of earthworms 20 years to create. It really wasn't until I spent some time working overseas that I became fully aware of the poverty of many soils compared to our own. It takes hundreds of years of seasonal flooding to build up the precious silts and other organic matter that form the soil.

With difficult soils we need to learn how to manipulate the environment to either work with the natural patterns or turn them in our favour. But with good loams, volcanic soils and silts we need to take great care and management to maintain their condition and keep them growing, to prevent deterioration or erosion.

SHADE AND SOIL

MY OWN GARDEN'S BEAUTIFUL volcanic ash is similar in quality to a silt in terms of particle size and fertility. What has fascinated me as I've watched my garden grow and change over the years is how the soil has grown and changed at different paces, depending on the planting. At the back, the trees provide canopy and cover and the leaf drop is high. I remove cabbage-tree and puka leaves mainly because they look big and messy, but I leave most others to mulch the soil. I do mulch and add sheep pellets through periods of idle gardening, but generally the soil is left to its own.

At the front, there are open lawn areas and less canopy. Where the ground is shaded and leaf litter is constant, the growth of organic matter is fast. Despite large trees, the gradient and the permeability of the soil still allow growth beneath and the

soil is becoming richer and moister. Where the soil is more
exposed, its structure remains that of beautiful volcanic ash
but the growth of organic content is less. Because the soil has a
scoria content any organic matter holds beautifully, but without
it the soil is so free-draining that it is developing at a slower rate.
While this is not a controlled experiment, it does indicate that
retention of clean, moving water is as essential to the growth of
organic matter beneath the ground as it is above. As experienced
gardeners will know,
a garden becomes less
dependent on watering
as it grows. Shade is one
aspect that reduces water
loss. While my section

> Clean, moving water is as essential
> to the growth of organic matter beneath
> the ground as it is above.

is verdant and green, my neighbours' section, which is cleared
and relatively untended, is dry and parched. Yet it is noticeably
greener along the boundary to our section where it receives more
shade in the morning than it does across the rest of the slope.
I would love to say this was because of my attentive gardening
spilling over the fence, but my garden is more a free spirit than a
sculpture and it is barely watered, even at the heart of summer.

TREES

TREES ARE THE FIRST TO PROVIDE shade in a garden and their
relationship with soil is cyclical. Beneath a young tree the soil
development is fast. As the roots push through the soil, fruits, flowers

and leaves drop. Birds and mammals gather in the branches, creating nests that fall at the end of spring, feasting on fruits, nuts and berries, and leaving behind their own castings at the base of the tree. As trees grow upwards the soil beneath changes again as the roots spread out and down, pulling most available water and nutrients from the ground beneath. On the trunks, mosses, lichen and fungi attach, creating moist spots where travelling seeds can find good growing conditions. Epiphytic plants attach to the branches. In New Zealand forests astelias, mistletoe, rata and ferns cover the branches of ancient trees, hanging down like green cloaks from these forest elders. By the time a tree reaches the end of its lifetime and falls to the forest floor it is already hosting an ecology of its own. At this point the soil beneath is likely to be poor; the large roots of the tree have processed the litter of the forest and redistributed it through this upper system. Not only does the tree's collapse bring light to the forest floor again, but its wood provides a mass of stored carbon. Fungi, water and moss are essential in turning this timber into soil. This is why untreated wood can be such a valuable source in the revitalisation of soil and the development of under-canopy planting. When revegetating bush areas, it is common for people to clear out old manuka and kanuka as they come to the end of their life. This timber may have other values for firewood or fencing, but some should be preserved for the bush floor. On sloping sites it is also a valuable method of informal terracing that will help hold mulch to the earth and allow the soil to rebuild its organic body.

SOIL AND NUTRIENTS

A BEAUTIFUL SILT OR LOAM SOIL is a gardener's delight for growing just about anything. However, if food production is the desired outcome it is important to understand more about your

soil than just its structure. For the food we grow in our gardens to provide us with a range of nutrients that we need to be healthy, the nutrients must be accessible to the plants through the soil.

There are a few reasons a soil may be deficient in nutrients. One is that a number of minerals, such as iodine, zinc, selenium, magnesium, chromium and boron, are not naturally found in high quantities in New Zealand soils. Another reason for deficiency is the growth of the same plants or crop over a long period of time. Plants change soil make-up in two ways – by the nutrients they use to grow, and by the chemicals they can sometimes introduce into the soil. Negative feedback is the process of a plant inhibiting another plant's growth, and gives us a window into some of the complicated chemistry that occurs beneath the ground. Studies in forests have shown that the greatest reducer of a seed germinating is proximity to the parent plant. From this it can be assumed that the parent plant in many circumstances releases a hormone that inhibits its seeds from competing with it directly. This is not the only example of how a plant's root system can control the make-up of the soil beneath. Eucalyptus has been shown in several scientific studies to cause the quality of soil to degrade and become very acidic (an acidity of 4.5, when the norm is between 5 and 7). This is because of the amount of calcium that the eucalypts pull from the soil. This shows how the overuse of one nutrient cannot just result in a lack but can actually change the natural state of a soil.

> Plants change soil make-up in two ways – by the nutrients they use to grow, and by the chemicals they can sometimes introduce into the soil.

OPPOSITE, ABOVE LEFT
Moss grows on living
wood, giving plants like this
epiphytic fern a spongy
layer that retains water
and nitrogen.

ABOVE RIGHT Epiphytes
such as these *Astelia*
cover trees so the
tree becomes its own
ecosystem.

BELOW Epiphytes will
outlive their hosts in many
cases, making use of the
wood once it falls to the
ground.

MAINTAINING FERTILITY

ONE OF THE MOST IMPORTANT LESSONS we can learn from
history is how even the greatest soils can be eroded or lost over
time if they are not maintained. A good gardener needs to be
constantly vigilant as to the health of their soil and be aware of
its subtle differences and changes. These lessons apply to all
soils, not just the best, and can be considered good practice for
all gardeners.

SOIL ACIDITY

IN NEW ZEALAND OUR SOILS have a healthy pH range between
5 – the most acidic – and 7 being more alkaline. The acidity of
the soil can alter the way nutrients are available in the soil, so
some plants that have really high nutrient need are inclined to
prefer a more acidic soil. Furthermore, as our understanding of
the world beneath increases, it is believed that part of the reason
that different plants thrive at different pH levels is because of
beneficial fungi that work symbiotically with root systems in
capturing and producing nutrients. High acidity is anything less
than 5.2, though it is uncommon to find New Zealand soils with
a pH lower than 5. In these conditions acid-loving plants such
as blueberries, camellias and rhododendrons thrive. Vegetable
gardens, on the other hand, tend to like a less acidic soil, which
is why your grandparents probably used to throw lime on the
vegetable garden after a harvest.

Hydrangeas are an easy way to check your soil pH. Those
who struggle to keep hydrangeas blue have a more alkaline soil,
while beautiful deep blues that don't lessen over the years are a
sign of acidity.

SOIL TESTING

YOU CAN GET YOUR SOIL ACIDITY tested so you know where it sits in the range, particularly if you want to grow acid-loving plants. If you Google 'soil tests' you will get a range of labs that can help you, but make sure you are clear what you would like them to test for. If you are going to go to the effort to test for acidity in a lab, you should definitely test for nutrients and trace elements as well.

A pH test can be done using reasonably simple tests available at the garden centre, too, so don't be afraid to give it a go yourself. It is likely you did a similar test at school if you did sciences.

If you want your soil tested for diseases, this is a different scenario as a lab would normally like you to specify what you are looking for so they can grow the offending pathogen in the right conditions. It is also a more expensive and time-consuming process, so patience is important and you should begin to treat your garden immediately.

SOIL DISEASES

IF YOU BELIEVE YOU HAVE A DISEASE in your soil it is likely to be a *Phytophthora*. There are different variations of this disease, but they attack plants in quite a distinct way. Because the *Phytophthora* moves through water in soil, its pattern of infection does not seem to have any rhyme or reason when observed from above. You will notice individual plants dying quite randomly, while healthier plants either side are prospering. This most often occurs in monocultures such as hedges or crops of potatoes and tomatoes. In fact, it was *Phytophthora* that was responsible for the potato famine in Ireland.

In the landscape *Phytophthora* often occurs next to a hard concrete area, such as a drive, where ground roots are excessively hot. There is also a relationship between outbreaks of *Phytophthora* and unmonitored irrigation that is left on for extended periods or during rainfall, especially in hotter months. It is less common in mixed plantings, and some plants are definitely more susceptible than others. *Phytophthora* also has different species which attack different hosts. Once a plant has an infection such as this it is very unlikely to recover and should be dug up, and when dealing with *Phytophthora* in crops you need to rest the soil for ideally a couple of seasons or more and plant with plants that are not of the same family so they won't carry the disease on. It is most common in clay soils that have been compacted during construction or where drainage and permeability are an issue.

The most effective defence is soil health and improving drainage, and if you have irrigation it is advisable to turn it off and allow the ground to dry out. In gardens with recurrent problems it is advisable to also introduce beneficial fungi. Trichoderms are fungi that are used by growers to protect young seedlings from root rot. If introduced to the soil at planting they will form a protective web around the roots that is defensive against *Phytophthora*. In existing plantings they can be laid as pellets around the plant and can help prevent healthy plants from developing problems. Trichoderms are sometimes sold as biofungicide.

MAGNESIUM

MAGNESIUM IS ANOTHER NUTRIENT that is commonly deficient in soils but is very important in plant growth. A magnesium deficiency often shows up in yellow leaves, most noticeably in super-hungry plants such as citrus and gardenias. It is easily added in the form of Epsom salts, but specialty fertilisers for citrus or tonics for gardenias also have good doses of magnesium in them. For general garden areas, dolomite lime is lime with a natural magnesium content. This is the best for compost and vegetables, as it both tempers acidity and enriches with magnesium. Dolomite lime is not, however, useful for gardenias, which like acid-rich soil. Gardenias need not just magnesium but lots of organic matter to keep the soil rich. Sheep pellets once a month from spring until autumn will give you prize specimens.

FERTILE SOIL AND CLEAN WATER

THE RELATIONSHIP BETWEEN SOIL AND WATER is extremely important. As New Zealand awakens to the current condition of our waterways, it is worth taking the time to look at how these systems are connected to our soil reserves and their lasting fertility. There is a relationship between farming slopes with grazing animals and soil loss. This is not to say that sloping land has no agricultural value, but history has taught us it is most sustainably farmed using terracing. It is quite easy to spot land that is eroding, as it is marked with lines of clay as the topsoil slips from its surface. Replacing soil in these areas is problematic because pasture struggles to grow on the clay, worms cannot survive, and therefore the process of natural soil growth is stunted. Revegetation does recover soils over time, but it is a slow process.

Ideally we need to avoid the initial damage to hillsides by looking at other ways of farming. Many farmers are now looking at reverting steep areas of ground either by retiring marginal land into bush reserves, or reallocating the land's use into forestry blocks. As the soil slips from slopes, this erosion can build momentum and further strip soil from lower pastures. Once soil

OPPOSITE Planting along
waterways helps to filter
and collect sediments and
excess nutrients. Flooding
redistributes silts onto
surrounding soil banks.

is in our waterways, some may be redistributed as silt through
flooding, but a large proportion of these valuable reserves are
washed out to sea for good.

A technique that is being increasingly used by farmers
and lifestyle-block owners to capture this soil is to plant next
to waterways and fence them off. Where planting is developed
along waterways, run-off from pasture – be it topsoil or nitrogen –
is slowed and some, if not all, is captured by the riparian plantings.
The expense required to invest in the initial plantings is worth it for
the farmer who wants to gain long-term benefits to the productivity
of the land as well as maintain the long-term value of their land-
holding. These riparian plantings are of greater importance now
that New Zealand has lost most of its wetland areas. Wetlands are
like slow natural filter systems that collect the soils and minerals
from the land as water travels through our water systems. They
create wonderful stockpiles of rich organic soils (which is why
they are so readily drained for agriculture), and we can learn much
about how to manage soils from the way wetlands work. While not
everyone has streams on their site, many of us are faced with water
issues or flood areas that may come and go with the wetter seasons.
Drainage of these areas is one option; but you should also consider
if there is value in directing this water through the garden, rather
than out into the stormwater. If you can slow these seasonal flushes
of water through appropriate planting it will assist in the growth of
your soil in these areas. Plants with strong vertical taproots such as
mamaku (black treefern) and nikau are wonderful for these zones.
Even quite a torrent of water will skirt around these narrow plants
rather than disturbing the root system.

When dealing with erosion from water-grazing animals or wind, understanding root systems is important to getting the right plants to manage the soil. Rocks can also be used to help slow and filter the water if you have an available source and access is not a problem. Make sure to encourage the water to wind gently rather than in a torrent. Most councils have a list of small shrubs and grasses that are ideal for riparian planting, and using local lists is important as it increases diversity and ensures hardiness. Do take the time to visit plant experts and explore new and different varieties other than the usual suspects. This can assist in the preservation of species and broaden diversity – the key to healthy systems. The plants you select should be able to handle both flooding and dry conditions. As part of a general approach, each wet garden created can greatly reduce the loss of soil and improve the quality of our waterways.

THE SACRED COW

DAIRYING IS AT THE HEART of our agricultural industry, and, while it's likely that we'll see more diversification as markets change, we still face many concerns over the impact of the urine and manure that are leaching into waterways. In India, however, traditional and organic farmers treasure cows' manure and urine as a valuable resource. Many farmers have cows that are kept only for manure production. The cow patties are used for a variety of products, including mosquito repellents, cooking starters and for insulating house walls and floors. Of greatest value, however, is

the manure, which is used to both maintain high soil fertility and to turn poor soils back into productive land. *Amrut pani* is the Indian name for this soil conditioner.

The idea of farming cows just for their effluent would turn the heads of most farmers in New Zealand, but it could be that overlooking manure is passing by a potential new cash cow just waiting to be milked. It could supplement falling milk prices, deal with pollution and build valuable soil reserves for future diversification in the farming sector.

Rajendra Thakkar runs 70 acres of organic farmland, supplying the city of Mumbai with high-grade organic produce, and he has 35 cows run specifically for soil management.

Rajendra Thakkar runs 70 acres of organic farmland, supplying the city of Mumbai with high-grade organic produce, and he has 35 cows run specifically for soil management.

They graze primarily on rice paddy fields after cropping. His recipe for liquid fertiliser contains a secret and sweet ingredient called jaggery. Jaggery is a concentrated product of palm sap, cane juice or dates and is used in cooking all through Asia and Africa. It is basically unrefined sugar, and is a healthier option in cooking than the white cane crystals so often found in organic food stores. For every 10 litres of manure Thakkar adds 10 litres of urine and 100 grams of jaggery. This is mixed together and left for three days until it begins to foam and ferment. It is then diluted with 10 parts of water and applied to all crops once every two weeks. The fertiliser is applied three times on the same day so that the soil absorption is maximised.

To prepare new gardens, dry matter such as leaves and twigs and some virgin soil from the planned garden are layered in a composting area. This is soaked in the *amrut pani* and left for a month and a half to break down. It is then spread at a thickness of 400–600mm over the surface of the soil and left for about three weeks to give time for worms and microbes to soak into the soil beneath. The final step in the process is to sow a starter seed mix into the ground. This seed mix contains a great diversity of plants – sweets, sours, hot leaves, herbs and flowers are mixed together and sown randomly over the whole site. After 45 days the whole crop is cut down by half. Half of this harvest is taken to be composted for the next soil mulch and the other half is chopped and dropped to directly mulch the ground. Thakkar repeats this process three times before he uses the land for production. After this, he says, you can grow any food crop on any piece of land.

The mixture of plantings is acknowledging the effect that different plants' processes beneath the soil have on creating a balanced and fertile system. By growing this diverse mix of plants directly sown into the ground you are ensuring that the soil has all of these benefits in balance.

One word of advice from Thakkar, though, is that New Zealand cows may not have as highly concentrated urine as a good Indian cow. Indian cows sweat more than cows in New Zealand, and so their urine is more concentrated. It may take New Zealand farmers a while to get breeding on track for cows that deliver at both ends.

PLANTING

PLANTING IN GOOD GROUND is a gardener's joy. In Maori
tradition we must say a karakia before we open Mother Earth,
asking her permission and thanking her for her gifts. This ancient
rite reflects a deep understanding of what is at work beneath the
surface. More and more research affirms that the more disruption
a soil undergoes, the more its fertility is disturbed. Modern
fertilisers give us quick-fix solutions to mask some of the stress
we are putting on soils, but there is no substitute to healthy soil to
ensure plant performance over a sustained period.

In revegetation work, clearing pasture before planting has
a lower strike rate than slit planting. Slit planting is suitable for
small nursery-raised plants, where you do as little as push the
spade into the soil and force the soil open, slide the plant in and
press the soil back around the base of the plant. As long as you get
the level of the roots correct, this method works beautifully. It
is also excellent for planting bulbs into the soil, especially those
you may be planting in large numbers, such as daffodils through
an orchard to assist in pollination. Slit planting causes very little
disruption to the surrounding soil. Planted in a good soil at the
start of autumn, little else should be necessary. For bigger plants,
cut a capital letter 'I' into the pasture and pull back each side.
Place the plant in the cut and push back the turf. It will mound
back over the plant's roots a little, but as long as it's clear of the
stem the plant should do well.

If a site has been cleared already, bark mulch is the next best
alternative and should be applied straight after planting. When

planting in the soil, take account of the mulch and keep the plant slightly proud of the soil so the mulch doesn't come too high around the stem or trunk of the plant.

TE KAINGA MARIRE

GARDENERS VALDA POLETTI AND DAVE CLARKSON have used their love of nature to transform a weed-ridden half-acre into a garden of international significance – Te Kainga Marire, in New Plymouth, which hosts one of the best collections of native plants in a domestic setting I've ever seen. While some of us sit upon these resplendent soils and simply bask in the generosity of nature, Poletti and Clarkson are the true botanists who instead use their advantage to learn more about the secrets of the natural world and its processes. Together they've crafted the most beautiful moss paths through groves of tree ferns, and created underground tunnels within the garden so that they can grow native orchids. New Zealand's native orchids are so small and delicate that most growers will advise you they are unsuited for the domestic garden.

The more we take the time to observe the world around us, be it the earth beneath our feet or what springs forth from it, the easier it becomes to work with it and create wondrous outcomes.

If you have good soil to build upon, you can focus on the eccen-

OPPOSITE This exposed
earth bank has been
covered in coconut fibre
matting before planting to
create an inexpensive and
stable green wall.

tricities of individual plants and the aspects they need to grow.
Poletti and Clarkson's garden is one of mimicry – not of other
gardeners, but of the wonders of a Jurassic flora whose beauty
is not blousy but is effortlessly abundant. Poletti and Clarkson's
knowledge and understanding of our native fauna comes from
decades of exploring the various landscapes in which these plants
grow naturally. This is the key to any gardener's success: observation
and appreciation. The more we take the time to observe the world
around us, be it the earth beneath our feet or what springs forth
from it, the easier it becomes to work with it and create wondrous
outcomes.

WEED MATS

WHERE YOU HAVE FERTILE SOIL, the complaint is often not what
you can grow but problems with the competition: weeds. Weeds
will turn up wherever there is good soil and water, and where there
are weeds people will look for a quick fix to save time and energy.

I never use plastic weed mat. As one landscaper joked to me
recently, weed mat is the most awesome product as long as you
don't use it in the garden. I'm more open-minded about organic
mattings that are designed to allow water to permeate and which
biodegrade over a few years. Some made with a wool base are
very effective in establishing large areas of planting, such as those
along motorways, where maintenance must be at a minimum.
These types of matting breathe. The plastic mats, however, even
the woven ones, can turn perfectly good soil bad. They also fail to

lessen weeds in the long run unless they are left bare. When the weed mat is mulched with pebbles, the soil that ceases to grow beneath the matting to feed your plants begins to grow instead in the cracks and crevices above the mat. Weed seeds gather here, too, and this creates a perfect environment for germination. The seeds' small roots are able to weave into the matting and the soil below as they grow. This produces weeds with a deep tap root that is near impossible to remove without chemicals, or removing the pebbles and matting and digging down. If you use bark as a mulch on top of the matting the problem is similar, except the bark breaks down and becomes a thin soil layer above the mat. Without the matting this is very beneficial, but with the weed mat in place its benefits are wasted on whatever seeds fall into this top layer. In a nutshell, use weed mat only where you have no desire to have any soil quality: it is best used beneath paths or on a greenhouse floor.

There are, of course, exceptions to any rule. Strawberries love black plastic snuggled against their rows. It is also great in nurseries beneath potted rows of plants – but not in the garden.

In the absence of any weed mat, plant thickly and mulch.

LOCATION, LOCATION, LOCATION

KATE GRACE, A YOUNG HORTICULTURALIST WORKING in Australia, compares the gardens she works on in the Australian bush to those that sit within her local river system in terms of fertility. For all her skills as a gardener, the advantages in working on a site where the soil has been delivered by centuries of floods are indisputable. River systems are sites where soil is likely to be most fertile, and are a good place to look for silty soils.

Australia is a diverse country with many climates and soil types. Even in the driest areas, where there is a river your chances of hitting the jackpot are good. While areas next to rivers are prone to flooding, these floods bring valuable silts to the earth. When looking for these precious silken soils, consider not just the path of a river but where it may have wound itself many centuries before. Rivers move, and they leave behind them soil reserves that are often the finest of them all. While loams are more common, pure silt is gardeners' gold. Sometimes it's not about growing soil, it's about hunting down the best site for the garden or enterprise you have in mind. If you are considering agricultural dependence, make sure you understand the soil you are working with and its limitations. Whatever the location, if beneath is black gold your chances of success are doubled.

> The advantages in working on a site where the soil has been delivered by centuries of floods are indisputable.

INGREDIENTS GUIDE

SHEEP PELLETS

The combination of wool and manure feeds a fertile soil, providing all the adequate nutrients to maintain a soil's growth.

MULCH

Mulches help to protect soils that have been cleared for planting, while also reducing water loss and competition from weeds.

LAWN CLIPPINGS

High in nitrogen, grass can be used in thin layers as a mulch around woody trees and shrubs.

PEA STRAW

A good, soft mulch suitable for vegetables or fast-growing greens. It contains additional nitrogen which helps feed the soil as well as protect it and as it breaks down it helps aeration. Lay over exposed earth.

BIOCHAR

Can be dug through the soil at planting, added to compost or used as a mulch over plants. Should be used with organic matter.

DOLOMITE LIME

Ideal for compost, helping to balance manures and food waste. Fruitflies are a sign of acidity, so their appearance means you need more lime. Dolomite contains magnesium, which is essential to plant and human health. Sprinkle sparingly, like icing sugar.

TRACE ELEMENTS

Trace elements are an important component in soils used for food production. They are contained in quality fertiliser and are also present in paramagnetic rock. Soil testing helps to identify deficiencies and correctly amend soils.

LEAF MULCH

Leaves can be collected and allowed to compost on new beds or used to create leaf mould to mulch beds in spring and autumn.

COMPOST

The more you harvest, the more important it is to replace organic matter. A vegetable garden especially produces abundantly through warmer months, and if these nutrients are not restored the soil becomes tired.

HEDGE TRIMMINGS

As well as direct application, hedge trimmings make a good addition to compost. A pile next to your compost allows you to add a layer of hedge trimmings between food scraps, keeping a compost aerated.

PLANTING APPROACH

Preserving soil is important when your soils are in good condition. Avoid intensive farming or gardening on slopes, and choose perennial plants over annuals.

Avoid clearing soils if possible, especially where rainfall is high or sun exposure is intense.

Retain organic matter in your garden's cycle. What you prune and remove should be returned to the soil, directly or through composting.

Consider adding sugar or fermenting fruits to your soil, especially alongside compost, as food for microbes.

Sand soils

When we think of sand we think of the coast and building castles, of summer memories of long days in and out of the sun and sea, and climbing on the limbs of pohutukawa trees. Sand follows us everywhere. A day at the beach brings it into our bed sheets, car seats and the pages of a summer read. Its fine particles are almost magnetic, transferring from one surface to the next, leaving a trail of summer through our cars and houses.

SAND IS FOUND NOT ONLY on the salty shores or at the edge
of dunes. Many good soils have a content of sand and, while
gardening in a sandy soil is full of challenges, it also has high value
in commercial horticulture. The fine pumice sands of the Waikato
have qualities that are treasured and sought after.

Sand moves like a liquid, and it is as fluid in its nature beneath
the earth's surface as it is above. This is the challenge of gardening
in the sand; it is land on the move, and plants fighting to lock their
roots onto something fight a losing battle, like arms reaching into
the darkness trying to grip onto a dream. Plants that grow naturally
in the sand are often movers themselves. Think of the spinifex that
dance along the coast, flying from shore to shore across beach and
through surf, or the running grasses that snake through the surface
with roots that are as comfortable moving horizontally as they are
moving into the depths of a soil. Even trees that occupy this territory,
like our beautiful pohutukawa, have aerial roots that can seek out
water and nutrients despite moving soils. A collapsing cliff does
not mean the demise of such a great tree; instead, its roots slowly
reanchor over time as the tree bends in the earth. Even the flax and
toetoe with strong deep root systems have a fluidity to them, bending
and moving with the same winds that mould and form the land.

SOIL APPROACH

GARDENING IN THIS TERRITORY IS LIKE trying to snag a
snapper: you need a hook and the right bait. To garden successfully
you need to find a way of latching onto the organic matter and

somehow creating an island of earth among soil that will otherwise be on the move. Even as you begin to create a structure in the soil – which is best created by the roots of plants – you also need a dependable supply of water and the ability to capture and best utilise this water when found.

With many sandy soils, proximity to the sea adds the further challenge of salt. Salt is capable of burning plants and is even used by some gardeners as a weedkiller, such is its toxicity. The amount of salt in a sandy soil relates not just to proximity to the coast but also to the amount of rainfall in your region. In a garden where rain is heavy and frequent, salt levels are not such an issue but salt spray from winds can still burn some plants.

Salt levels are not likely to be a problem in sandy soils that drain freely. They can become a problem with intensive irrigation of soils where the water sits only on the surface so any salts in the water build up in the top layer of soil over time. This requires an improvement in drainage to leach the salts away, which then requires more irrigation and fertiliser. Salination is quite a distinct issue to salt spray on plants in a coastal situation.

Salt at the coast can also occur near tidal estuaries. If you are unsure how exposed your garden is to salt, the best test is to identify the plants that are growing well in your local area and see how hardy they are.

Pumice is formed when frothy magna full of combustible gases cools faster than it can form a crystalline structure. This gives it two qualities which are very advantageous to gardeners. It is soft, which makes it easy for roots to push through as they grow, and it is full of air bubbles. This creates a wonderful surface in which organic matter can be captured, which is key to the development of topsoil. It is also more stable than most sands which have weathered more slowly and been polished along the way. This means the particles pack tightly in among each other, unlike coastal or river sand, which tends to easily shift with water and wind movement.

REUSING WATER

WATER ESCAPES FROM SAND, so we need to ensure we have a reliable and consistent source. The first port of call should be the management of wastewater and what we can collect from roofs and structures. While rainwater is probably the easiest to collect and manage, in periods of lower rainfall this source can also dwindle. You need to maintain large water reserves, so using bigger tanks is generally better. Wastewater storage is more difficult, mainly due to council restrictions in some areas.

A family of four, all taking a daily shower or bath, amounts to around 360 litres a day – or 2,520 litres a week. That's a lot of water when applied to a garden. Add to this your standard washing machine doing five washes a week, which is around 1,000 litres, and it comes to 3,520 litres of grey water from only two sources. The products most people use in their washing machines and showers are of no harm to a garden, and can in fact be best managed when slowly filtrated through a plant's roots. Soaps are actually a common ingredient in many potting media, and assist in water distribution through a soil.

To build up organic matter in a soil you need root systems that can create a structure or web beneath the ground capable of stabilising the soil but also holding organic matter within its system. It is best to create a system where water is supplied infrequently and deeply. This encourages roots to have to grow deeply and become strong. It is a fine line between spoiling and sustaining a plant.

Many argue that if a plant can't survive without irrigation then it is not suited to a site, while others will happily spoil the child to

create the desired oasis. My opinion sits in between. In areas such as the north of New Zealand I resist watering systems where possible. In many situations this is viable, but you need to take into account how restricted the plants' area of garden is and also the timing of planting. When a plant is young and has come from a garden centre in the heat of summer – where it is likely to have been receiving water daily – planting it out and leaving it to its own devices is certainly running a risk. The roots have developed to receive water in the pot on a regular basis, and are not able to immediately stretch deep into the soil where it is cool and there may be water reservoirs. If you do not water under these same circumstances then you are likely to face losses. It's true that the plants that do survive will be the hardiest to your conditions and so this is advantageous, but they have also not been given the best chance to adapt.

WHEN TO PLANT

IT IS OFTEN RECOMMENDED THAT YOU PLANT in late autumn when rain can be more consistent and lower temperatures mean there is less transpiration from both the plant's leaves and the ground itself. It will often appear that a plant has done nothing in that first season after planting. Sometimes trees or shrubs sit for years appearing to do little, but you must remember that there is more happening beneath than we can view. French designer James Basson talks of his frustration at short-lived lavender in well-nourished and watered gardens when in the wild the same lavenders flowered year upon year. The roots of these wild plants went metres into the ground through cracks within the rock. Efficient plants invest their energy beneath the ground before things stir above. Of course we have no window beneath, so it can be frustrating watching in hope that what you have is a slow-burner and not a non-performer.

If a plant has this cooler period in which to begin to develop its root system, by spring it is ready to develop some upper growth and will often perform very well.

In my opinion the desired point of planting depends on both the plant type and method of watering. Trees and shrubs must be encouraged to have deep roots. In dry areas they should be planted in autumn and watered as little as possible. In the first summer after planting, they should be watched in periods of drought and given lovely deep waterings less often. What must be avoided is lots of consistent surface watering that keeps the plant's roots shallow and weak. Watering a garden in dry periods has quite a different impact on gardens than intensive industrial-scale irrigation systems, and they should not be confused.

WHEN TO WATER

A VEGETABLE GARDEN IS A GOOD EXAMPLE of plants worth watering. If you think about the volume of water you are taking from a garden during harvest periods, to put some in at the driest points is common sense. The first summer after planting is also when we need to watch plants for water. My preference is always to water plants as they need it, rather than the plants becoming dependent on a watering system. Sometimes the scale of planting

means even an occasional water is simply not practical by hand. In these cases the most common watering system is a soaker hose that deeply saturates the soil rather than spraying water around freely. Even if the hose is on an automated system, frequency is important. No garden needs to be always wet; this can actually cause an increase in soil-borne disease such as *Phytophthora* (although in sandy soils this is one concern you won't have!).

PATHS AND PAVING

WHEN PAVING AN ARID GARDEN, you need to think of your paths and patios not purely as places to sit and survey, but as water features designed to collect and flood the desired areas of your garden. A good landscaper will always slope the paving away from the house to ensure there are no problems with dampness. In an arid garden this can be taken a step further. If you work out the amount of water that is falling off hard surfaces there is no reason why this should not be captured and directed into your garden. The simplest step is to make sure any slope is directed towards garden areas. A path that sits slightly above the level of the garden will further encourage run-off into garden beds. In Japanese gardens, clay gutters are used not only on roofs but through the gardens to redistribute collected water more evenly throughout. If your roof water is not being collected into a tank it can be directed into garden areas through a series of flood zones and rills. This basic system is commonly called a 'rain garden' and in dry areas it is an efficient way of redistributing water through a garden.

OPPOSITE ABOVE This desert garden by Steve Martino uses shade to protect the gardens beneath and raises hard surfaces above the soil so excess water feeds into the soil.

OPPOSITE BELOW Mulching with stones helps prevent sandy soil moving in hot windy conditions.

Taking this idea in another direction altogether is the very small and low-budget Crack Garden in San Francisco. The project cost just $500 to implement. The garden transformed what was otherwise a bland concrete carport into an award-winning garden using little more than a jackhammer, some soil and some seeds. The concrete was hammered to create even and regular lines which were then filled with soil and sown with wildflower seed. This is a wonderful example of how a small window of opportunity between the earth and an urban landscape above is enough for life to recover.

ADDING CLAY

WHILE SANDY SOILS ALLOW WATER TO PERMEATE, they lack what clay soils have – the ability to hold water. Lovely organic compost can quickly slip through a sandy soil, whereas clay is sticky and will bind even with a smooth sand particle. While too much clay is problematic, as with all soils we are looking to create a balance, and mixing anywhere from 20 to 40 per cent clay into a sandy soil can help to initiate this process. Mixing the clay with compost, existing soil and sheep pellets in a wheelbarrow before planting will create a great starter mix.

Digging a hole in very sandy soils can itself be a problem; the hole fills as fast as you can dig it. This is easier in wet periods as sand is more stable, but in some sandy gardens even in the wettest months the water doesn't stick around for long. If you are able to dig a hole, line the base of it with newspaper and then a mulch, such as straw, sphagnum, bark or dried-out hedge prunings. Other ideas are twiggy driftwood, sheep dags, banana leaves or unwanted paperback books. Be creative and work with materials you have on hand. Some ash or charcoal from the fire is also appropriate to add as it is stored carbon. The clay and compost mixed into the sandy soil will help the plants get started, and this drier mass will help hold the nutrients in this top layer as the roots strengthen. This then gives the roots something to grow into, as the upper layers are used for growth. As the garden grows, continued mulching and feeding from the top will help the soil grow from this point. It may be easiest to imagine that what you are doing is mulching top and bottom to help the formation of a topsoil layer. Once your plant creates a strong network of roots, this will help retain this soil and all the good things that come with it.

This will not change your soil substrata, and you will still need to consider plants that are able to handle drier conditions, but it will broaden what you can grow with more ease.

If digging down is not working, create what depth you can, line with a brown mulch layer, and then build the plants upward. When mounding, you still need to ensure that the finished level of the soil does not expose the plant's roots, or mound mulch or organic material around the trunk or stem of a plant. The mound should gently contour back. Because water retention is of such great importance in sandy soils, if possible create a corral around the raised planter, either with boulders or with driftwood. Bricks or old pavers are also appropriate if they are on hand.

SHELTER

WHEN GARDENING IN A SANDY ENVIRONMENT shelter is very important. Where water disappears quickly you want to create shade to cool the soil surface and reduce transpiration or evaporation. Creating shelter will also reduce wind, which will lessen the constant weathering of the soil's surface. Beneath the ground, too, you are building a wall of roots and you should not underestimate how much this can help contain water within the garden. While it can still disappear vertically, water flow on a horizontal plane will be slowed. By adding mulch to the surface you will further reduce the directions through which water can escape.

MULCHING

AS YOUR GARDEN BEGINS TO GROW, even the most leisurely of gardeners can create mulch. While there is definitely value in bringing in material from outside if your soil has a low organic content, if you are on a tight budget or isolated from a reliable source of introduced compost or mulch, then chop and drop is an easy and effective way to build soils. Instead of clearing away prunings you should chop them as you go and use the material to cover the soil. This can be around existing plantings you wish to keep healthy, or through new areas that you plan to plant or have just planted. As shelterbelts establish, you can borrow from these to build the soil within the garden, too. Keep in mind that woody material takes a longer time to break down than green materials such as annual crops and perennials, which feed the soil more quickly.

When chopping and dropping there are certain common-sense rules to follow. Watch out for diseased material. If you have had an outbreak in your garden of a soil disease or fungus, beware of spreading it through your soil. As a rule, diseased plant material should be hot-composted (see page 216), or removed from site. Problem insects, too, should be considered. While insects mainly feed on the live plants – and this is when you will be most aware of them – you'll often find them on the backs of leaves or in woody material over winter, so keep an eye on this, especially where you have had problems in a previous season. Take some time to research the life cycle of pests in your garden to see if they can live in leaf litter or soil. Generally, as the health of your soil improves, your garden

will find a natural balance and, like humans, when it is healthy its resilience to disease is greater; but hygiene also plays a part.

If chop and drop is too messy for your style of gardening, don't waste this valuable organic matter. In a compost system this bulk material helps keep the pile aerated and healthy. Compost is all about layers in the same way growing soil is. In the garden we can create these simple layers by applying blood and bone, sheep pellets and mulches, with lime applied as needed, composting straight to the earth.

NITROGEN-FIXING PLANTS

NITROGEN-FIXING PLANTS ARE WONDERFUL in any soil, but you can use them in sands both as starter crops and then, using the chop and drop system, to build fertile organic bulk into the soil or to add to compost which can be returned to the garden once matured. The amazing thing about nitrogen-fixing plants – many of which are legumes – is that the process of nitrogen production occurs because of a symbiotic (mutually beneficial) relationship between the plant's roots and a specific bacteria that lives within the root system. While nitrogen-fixing plants are particularly useful to us gardeners, bacteria of all sorts form these pairings with plants that are essential parts of the ecology of the soil.

Some of the best nitrogen-fixing plants are also excellent food crops. Beans and peas leave more nitrogen in the soil than what was there before, making them excellent crops to use if a plot is tired and depleted. Mustard, too, has long been used in agriculture to allow soils to rest, and can be sown over beds in winter months as a green mulch. Clover, alfalfa and lupins are examples of traditional crops grown for the health of our soils, but take care as they can spread into unwanted areas. Soybeans and peanuts contain nodules with these bacteria, called rhizobia, in their root systems. To gain the full benefits of nitrogen-fixing crops after harvest, the plants need to be mulched. This can be done directly to the soil by the cut and drop method, or by composting.

ADDING FIRE

THE RELATIONSHIP BETWEEN FIRE AND SOILS is older than humanity itself. Many plants have evolved to be able to benefit from the processes that on the surface seem so devastating to all life. Yet nature has a way of creating new beginnings when all seems to be lost. Horticulturalists studying seeds of certain desert plants from Australia and Africa struggled with low germination rates in some species, which prevented propagation. That was until they observed the resurgence of growth after a fire, and so they tried a new trick – burning the seeds. Most gardeners know that to trick cold-climate plants such as tulips into flowering in areas where there are no deep freezes, we can lift the bulbs and store them in the freezer for a period in the winter. It is the opposite with seeds from areas which have a natural fire season. By throwing the seeds into the fire and then planting you will get a higher germination rate. It is stored in the DNA of the seed to wait until fire before it grows.

The Japanese have long used fire to preserve hardwoods from decomposition, using a surprisingly simple process of charring the outside of the timbers. After visits to Japan we adopted this process of heavily charring the inside of raised vegetable beds made from macrocarpa or totara, where the wood is in contact with the soil. The charring stabilises the carbon and protects it from rot by reducing the absorption of water.

For Australian Aboriginals, as with many other indigenous cultures, fire was used for many reasons, such as hunting and land management, but also as an important part of soil fertility. Interestingly it is not just humans in Australia who start fires; birds also have been shown to spread fire to drive food out of the trees. I have a friend who witnessed this first hand as they drove through the outback, and accounts are not uncommon of such events. The burnings resulted in a return of the biomass above ground into the earth, which favoured many of the plants that Aboriginals used for food. Fire patterns were used to increase the diversity of systems and therefore the range of foods available.

The majority of our food crops are most productive in open ground where competition for sun from trees is reduced. While it is good to understand how fire restores the soils, the disadvantage of mass burnings to clear land is the release of carbon into the atmosphere. The fire reduces the amount of biomass available to us to form new soil. Instead, when clearing land the scrub is a resource for soil production if nothing else; and burning is not an efficient way of managing this resource.

POTASH

POTASH HAS LONG BEEN CONSIDERED an important ingredient in soils. As the name suggests, it is traditionally made from the ash of burnt plant material which is then soaked in water in a pot. These days commercial potassium is gathered from ancient deposits that are mined from the earth. The white residue is used as a valuable source of potassium, which is essential to a plant's ability to absorb water as well as for the formation of flowers and fruits. Too much, though, can end up as salts in the soil, so it should always be applied with lots of organic matter, especially in sandy soils. It also makes the soil more alkaline (a higher pH), so is not favoured by acid-loving plants. You can simply add ash from your fire to your compost or to garden beds when you are composting and mulching. If you are using a good-quality commercial compost, though, it isn't needed, as these already have ideal quantities of potassium.

BIOCHAR

I WAS FIRST INTRODUCED TO CHARCOAL as a growing medium by two Singaporean orchid experts working in Japan. The majority of orchids in Singapore are grown in charcoal these days, rather than bark. In Japan, charcoal is also sometimes used as a mulch around plants and in gardens. Charcoal on its own has value, but when charged with nutrients and microorganisms it becomes a very stable growing medium. In this state it's known as 'biochar', and is considered a valuable soil conditioner. Biochar can be produced by burning charcoal (see following pages for further details), and is technically charcoal inhabited by fungi and microorganisms which enable plant health and soil growth and are highly beneficial to soil. It creates permeability in a soil, but also hosts these beneficial fungi and microorganisms. Modern biochar is produced so that it releases as little gas into the atmosphere as possible, so as not to contribute to pollution or global warming.

The origins of biochar, though, are not in Asia but come from the discovery of deposits of rich *terra preta* soil in the Amazonian basin. The discovery of these soils was important because naturally occurring Amazonian soils are surprisingly very poor, with most of the nutrients held in the tropical forests above. Attempts to clear and farm this land on a large scale have frequently failed and been abandoned; the high rainfall has quickly leached away any remnant topsoil and nutrients. On a smaller scale, indigenous farmers create small clearings by slashing and burning within the forest. These are managed for short periods and then abandoned for a new area when the fertility drops. The *terra preta*, however, are different. These black soils grow around 1 centimetre a year in depth, which is the same rate as pasture with earthworms, and are one of the best examples of a living soil. Analysis of the *terra preta* soils shows that they contain human and animal excrement, pottery, plant biomass which is essentially compost, food waste such as bones, shells and husks, and biomass from water plants, primarily algae. While most of these ingredients are commonplace in soil production, there is one other ingredient that is of most interest – and that's the partially burnt charcoal, or biochar. It not only provides a tool for soil amendment, it is also being explored around the world for its ability to capture stable carbon reserves. Traditionally, it's unlikely that the charcoal was specifically inoculated with bacteria; it's even possible that the charcoal was originally used to reduce the odour of sewage, rather than manure being added to activate the charcoal for growth.

It is also possible that the use of charcoal came about

through the production of ceramics. Large amounts of broken pottery are found in *terra preta* soils, and, while it also is likely that this pottery assists the quality of the soil (as discussed earlier, terracotta has high value in many areas of horticulture), the production of pottery requires the high temperatures and low-oxygen burning that are ideal for the production of charcoal. As this waste product was added to the soil, it is likely the benefits were learnt and passed from community to community, resulting in these pockets of fertile soil throughout the Amazon. The charcoal reduces the leaching to such a degree that rather than soil loss these soil reserves continue, even when not managed, to grow.

Biochar not only provides a tool for soil amendment, but it is also being explored around the world for its ability to capture stable carbon reserves.

There is a lot of confusion concerning the difference between charcoal and biochar. The simplest way of explaining it is that while biochar is charcoal, not all charcoal is or can be used as biochar. Charcoal suitable for use as a biochar must contain no additives. Many charcoals on the markets, especially bricks, contain glue additives that assist in the binding of the dust, making them easier to use.

To create a biochar the charcoal should only be charred organic matter, and needs to be activated by soaking in a liquid fertiliser or simply by adding it to compost. Microorganisms thrive in this material, which is one of the reasons biochar is so good for soil conditioning. It is even under investigation for disease control in ash die-back in England, where ash trees are being injected with the biochar with some promising results.

The production of charcoal for biochar purposes is done under strict conditions; the waste timber is burned in an enclosed environment which helps produce an ashless charcoal. The charcoal should be pure black both outside and within, and makes a pleasant tinkling sound when it's poured. There are many helpful videos on the internet on biochar production, if you have time and space and want to give it a go. Be aware, though, that if you are purchasing your own charcoal to create biochar you should make sure you know that it is produced from waste or a sustainable timber source, that the gases are well confined in the production, and that it is has no additives that might impede the growth of microorganisms.

If you have charcoal left behind in a fire, it definitely has value to your soil. If you separate the ash from the charcoal you can soak the charcoal in a good seaweed fertiliser and add it to food production beds or first to the compost.

Charcoal in a sandy soil helps to hold nutrients in microorganisms as well as organic matter, but it has been shown to be effective in soil growth whatever the substrata of soil you are managing.

PLANTING

PLANTS GIVE US SO MUCH INFORMATION about where they originate from, and understanding a plant's likely origin means we can also understand how suitable it is for a site. A sandy soil is inevitably both dry and exposed, which means that plants with a smaller and harder leaf are more suitable. Grasses also do very well in sandy soils; their immense root structures have the ability to grow into water reserves far beneath the surface.

In America, photographer Jim Richardson set to work with Dr Jerry Glover of the Land Institute in Salina, Kansas, to capture these extraordinary root systems. For a plantophile like myself, these images are pure beauty. They capture how much we take for granted by thinking that we know the plant above when beneath the ground these extraordinary structures exist that few people have ever seen. They also allow us to appreciate how important such plants are in preventing erosion, and how much carbon is held beneath the earth in these beautiful webs. Among the roots live microbes, fungi, worms and other insects in communities of great complexity. David Attenborough's revelations of the complexities of a simple ants' nest give us a window into these wonders. Beneath the cities we create are other worlds: ants have nurseries, waste areas, food stores. Their lives are organised not that differently from our own.

Not only do many plants have vast root systems beneath the earth that outweigh their mass above, but plants are more deeply connected with the soil beneath than they are with the land above. Seeds can lie dormant in the earth for thousands of years. Bulbs, rhizomes, tubers and corms remain below in winter periods or in periods of drought, waiting to show themselves until temperatures above are warmer or until the rains arrive.

It still surprises me (though it should not) how many plants

OPPOSITE Layering of
organic matter is essential
for soil growth.

come back with renewed vigour after pruning. Camellias, puka, olive trees and puriri are just a small number of the plants that will fight back with an abundance when cut back into old wood. It is a good reminder that so much of the plant's vitality is in the ground beneath. A good prune of old wood can give many trees a new lease of life. Remembering this and managing the size of your trees can help keep them productive and useful. Letting them grow unabandoned in a suburban setting can determine a tree's inevitable death as they begin to outcompete us for sun or views. If you are timid with the pruners when you look at the tree before you, take in its full size above and beneath the earth and you'll be more confident in reining in its spread above.

PLANTING WITH SEEDS

AS MUCH AS PLANTS NEED SOIL they also make and stabilise soil in their own interests. The quickest way to lose soil is to remove plants, and the fastest way to grow it, apart from composting, is through planting. A lot of research suggests that the most effective way to establish a garden in low-water situations is by using seed directly planted into the ground. Vegetable gardeners are well aware of the many plants that perform far better when sown directly into beds. Beans, peas and carrots and other root crops all take offence at having their roots disturbed during development. Lawns also do best when started from seed, as long as they are sown in spring or autumn when warmth and water are available in equal quantities to ensure the best start. Yet in our

ornamental gardens it's uncommon to landscape from seed. It is often recommended to plant younger plants so that the root system and top growth are of equal strength. This is excellent advice for revegetation and large gardens, but in smaller areas where privacy or shelter may be needed, or you may be keen to see a fruit tree become productive, there is an argument for larger specimens.

Planting directly with seed is not that commonly practised outside the vegetable garden, and yet it is not that difficult. The main battle in fertile soils is that, with plenty of nutrients and water available, competition is at its peak and weeds are likely to outperform the plants you attempt to sow, so most gardeners choose to plant bigger and mulch thickly. But in poorer sandy soils (and gravel soils, too), where competition is low, seed becomes a valid option. To give your seeds an advantage over other plants brave enough to approach an arid domain you could get inspiration from the guerrilla gardeners who are famous for reoccupying abandoned urban spaces with wildflowers and the use of seed bombs.

A lot of research suggests that the most effective way to establish a garden in low-water situations is by using seed directly planted into the ground.

Clay is a great antidote to sand, and is a key ingredient for a seed bomb. A basic recipe is one part clay, one part compost and one part seeds of your choice. If the mix is dry, add a little water or even some premixed seaweed fertiliser for a bit of extra nutrients and microbes. When selecting your plant species, make sure the seed is both hardy for your region and not a pest plant.

In a sand soil this could be lavender or globe artichokes or native *Pimelea* (New Zealand daphne), grasses, hebes or parahebes. Roll the mix together into small, hazelnut-sized balls and dry in the sun. They are then ready to plant. Planting in the wet season is always going to help your plants grow. It will also encourage lovely long root systems that stretch deep into the sandy soil following the path of water, unlike potted plants that have started out spoilt in rich mixes at the nursery.

As well as planting direct, if you are growing your own plants from cutting or seed, start them in a sandy mix, such as a cacti and succulent mix, rather than a regular potting mix. This will help them transition from pot to ground with greater ease.

PLANT SELECTION

GET OUT TO LOCAL NURSERIES and make use of their knowledge of local conditions. Plants grown for garden centres need to look fat and flowery to earn a place on the garden-centre shelves, in the same way as fruit and vegetables are often grown to look good at the supermarkets rather than to provide the best flavour. Instead, visit local nurseries and you will find a range of plants that are suited to your soils. Some growers, too, will grow local lines in poorer-quality mixes that are hardened to local conditions. They may not look as flash in the pot, but they tend to have greater resilience. If you are propagating plants yourself, take care to match the soils you're growing them in to the conditions of your garden. Your plants will start smaller but will be tougher and stronger as they grow.

All gardens have their pros and cons. Here in New Zealand, gardeners in the north look in envy at the apricots produced in the Hawke's Bay and the plump cherries, peonies and pachystegia (rock daisies) that thrive in the cooler winters of Marlborough. And, in the opposite direction, the leafy greens of Auckland and further north look to be an enviable solace against the drought-afflicted hills around the Canterbury Plains. Soil, too, is part of this game. We simply need to work out what our soil can do that others can't, and plan our gardens according to their strengths.

The more experienced a gardener you become, the more sense this will make to you, as the simplicity and complexity of gardening become the same. The key to being a good gardener is first observing the environment around you and then adapting yourself to it and it to you. It's a dance, and while you won't always have the same rhythm, as you step in and out of seasons you start to learn each other's habits and your moves increase in complexity. There are surprises and changes that keep you interested. A good gardener is like a good lover: they are not just there for one riotous season; they weather the storms, and find value as much in the fallen fruit as in those picked fresh or plucked and preserved.

HUGELKULTUR BEDS

HUGELKULTUR BEDS ARE ONE OF THE many interesting approaches used in permaculture practice. One of the important ideas of permaculture is working out how your garden fits into the systems that are already available around you, so if you wish to practise this style of soil management (which I highly recommend) you need to be keen and able to experiment within your locality. I don't believe in closed systems; our gardens are not islands. They will be visited by birds, winds and rains that come and go with or without our approval. It is common sense, though, to take care with the way you manage your own piece of earth and how that will affect the surrounding environment. Whatever waste can be put back into the earth should be done so. There are many gardens that, through a process of good design, have the capacity to compost the majority of their organic matter. As for what we add to our gardens, this too can be given careful thought, and one rule will not always fit all situations.

A hugelkultur bed is an example of a different way of building soil that could be modified in various ways to create other ideas of how to garden when the elements are against us.

Imagine a mound or low wall of firewood or fallen tree stumps. It could be manuka or pine or an old oak. The wood should be arranged so that it has good structure, and ideally the wood selected for this sort of garden should not be a hardwood like totara or macrocarpa, which will be slow to break down. Wood that has been fallen for a while and is already softening and hosting fungi is ideal. You could use burnt timbers at the core if there has been a fire, but while this will be good stored carbon for future soil health, you still need the soft wood to create fertility. Cover this wood mound with a topsoil or loam, then mulch and plant it immediately.

The first stage of planting should include perennial herbs and annuals as well as nitrogen-fixing legumes. This helps to stabilise

your topsoil. Shrubs and trees can be added in succession. The decomposing wood provides future nutrients and soil, but also helps the system retain water by acting like a very fine, slow sponge. The shape of your hugelkultur should consider all of the elements as with any garden – the direction of the sun and wind and the flow of water on-site – and should be tailored to fit these. While not every garden will have the room or require such a radical approach, using hugelkultur offers lots of benefits. Storing woody material beneath the ground helps retain water and develop soil over time. Fungi are the key in this process, and their importance to soil health is becoming increasingly clear. The more we learn about the soil beneath, the more we are coming to understand that fungi are essential to a healthy garden. Raising a garden up above difficult ground can make the most of a free-draining substrata while still building soil and reducing leaching. Contouring the land can create different microclimates and aspects that will improve growth.

GARDENS IN SAND SOILS

I REMEMBER WELL A DAY IN MOROCCO where I was travelling with the man who would one day become my husband. We had spent the night before travelling from Tangiers on the Marrakesh Express, and were exhausted but enthusiastic to discover the sites of Marrakesh. We combined his love of history with mine of gardens by clambering through the ruins of an ancient palace. The sandy walls had long been stripped of their once ornate tiles and stood bare and brown, yet in the midst of this abandoned structure

OPPOSITE ABOVE Water
reservoirs in an arid
environment are essential.

BELOW LEFT Water plants
such as *Apodasmia similis
oioi* help to filter water and
capture excess nutrients.

BELOW RIGHT Water
rill surrounded by
Muehlenbeckia astonii
and *Phormium cookianum*
at Daltons Plantation,
Matamata

the garden, with a grove of citrus, still thrived in the hot sun. The
tall walls and paths of this once-grand building were designed
to capture and funnel a continuous supply of water through a
complex system of stone pools and rills, fed also by a spring, into
the heart of this sunken garden. Among the trees a local gardener
was chasing a cobra that had decided to occupy this Garden of
Eden, a sanctuary that had survived centuries of looting and
neglect in this most arid environment. It was a very fine example
of how we can form architecture to create gardens that outlive
us. Walls provide shelter and shade that protect roots. Paving and
sunken gardens can be designed to capture and manipulate water.
The structures within a garden can be used not just to create a
modified environment for ourselves, but also for the plants upon
which we are dependent for shade, food and tranquillity.

We can learn a lot about working in sandy soils from designers
overseas who have long worked with various gravelly or low-nutrient
soils. In England, designers Gavin McWilliam and Andrew Wilson
restore chalk soils by adding a clay layer to the top. Clay, as we know,
is full of vital nutrients but lacks drainage, so they are fighting one
type of soil with the other. Limestone soils are not uncommon in
New Zealand either, and sit somewhere in treatment between gravel
and sand, so so adding clay also works here.

SANCTUARY IN SAND

AMERICAN STEVE MARTINO, LIKE MANY of the designers who
have found different ways to work within a landscape, takes his

inspiration not from books on the great gardens of the past, but by absorbing the lessons of nature. He studies life's ability to survive not just in rolling hills of sand but in the complex beauty and diversity that exists on what may appear barren to be on the surface. Martino does not believe in gardens that are attached to a lifeline of tubes and machines and regular doses of medication to be sustained. Instead, we should look for the life that is suited to the environment in which we work. This creates distinct gardens with the same uniqueness as the landscapes they occupy. If the garden is suited to the soil then there is little need for irrigation or constant attendance.

Once we understand how a soil system works we can modify it to expand the life it is able to sustain, but we need to do so in a manner which is relevant to the environment around us.

Instead of living mulches such as barks, Martino uses the local stones to prevent the fine soils from taking flight. He uses clay, too, to cover the earth. Buildings are mulched with cacti roofs. And yet his work is not just a replica of the natural world. Simple walls create shelter to cool the roots of the plants beneath, and water rills run through the garden in the style of ancient medina such as you might find in Spain or Morocco.

Capturing water in a garden provides a resource for ourselves and our gardens, and attracts birds. Watering a garden to give it relief in periods of dry is different to creating dependence. Our gardens are spaces where we nurture the wild, and they are our sanctuaries as landscapes unaffected by humankind

OPPOSITE ABOVE
American landscape
architect Steve Martino
works in harmony with
the existing environment,
bringing life to an
otherwise bare terrain.

OPPOSITE BELOW Using
stones to retain gardens
helps to keep organic
matter in the soil and
direct water.

become scarcer. By creating gardens that are not dependent on industrialised processes, we are protecting the plants that occupy them. If we have a drought or a petrol shortage, we want our gardens to be resilient so we can depend on them as much as they depend on us.

It is the job of the individual gardener to observe local conditions. Once we understand how a soil system works we can modify it to expand the life it is able to sustain, but we need to do so in a manner that is relevant to the environment around us. If you have sandy soil and a stony desert, go for a walk and take note of where the plants are appearing; take pictures of what is surviving, its manner and habits. If you sit within range of winter snows, learn how melting snow feeds the soils in spring. Look for that path of water beneath the earth and above, and lead your garden to it. Beside a river, find the silt beds and preserve them. On hills, beware of erosion and tread gently, planting to preserve the soils and reserve carbon. All around us are the answers to our own environment, and being responsive to this is how great gardens are made.

INGREDIENTS GUIDE

CLAY

The fine particles of clay help to retain water and nutrients in a sandy soil.

NEWSPAPER

Can be used to line planting holes and as a mulch to assist in holding nutrients and water.

WOOD

Creates slow reserves of brown material that will not slip through the sandy soil. Absorbs water as it slowly decays and adds organic matter to the soil.

MULCH

Reduces water loss and protects the soil beneath from oxidisation. It also reduces competition from weeds.

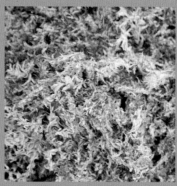

SPHAGNUM

Retains water around the roots of plants. Should be used sparingly.

SEAWEED

Chopped and used as a mulch or soil conditioner, seaweed retains water and adds nutrients to the soil.

HEDGE TRIMMINGS

Hedge trimmings and other prunings add organic bulk that can be used as a mulch and help with water retention.

BIOCHAR

Holds nutrients, microbes and moisture in the soil in a very stable state. Effective in creating stable living soil systems.

ROCK

Can be positioned beneath and above the ground to control the flow of water and therefore the accumulation of organic matter within a soil.

COMPOST

Rich organic matter is essential in changing a soil from arid to productive. It is essential for the introduction of important microbes and fungi that assist soil health.

LEAF MULCH

Leaves can be collected and allowed to compost on new beds, or used to create leaf mould to mulch beds in spring and autumn.

PLANTING APPROACH

Capture water any way you can. Even the footings of a stone wall will affect the flow of water to some extent. Buried half plastic bottles under a tree will capture some water. Space them to allow roots to move past them.

Start your garden with deep-rooting plants such as grasses. The roots stabilise the soil and create a fibrous network that retains organic matter, which in turn preserves water.

Digging down for garden beds in a sandy soil can be beneficial. Sunken gardens pool water and can reach into more stable soils.

Layer rich soil between newspaper to help prevent soil leaching through the sand. The newspaper breaks down as the plants' roots make their way through the soil.

Gravel soils

A gravel soil is easily identified. Its formation begins in a rocky landscape where weather and water slowly erode the rock over time to form smaller particles. At between 5 and 15 millimetres in size the rock can be defined as a soil. The type of rock you may have in your garden can vary greatly. It could be rough, white chalky limestone, or grey basalt rounded by river waters or ground down by the crashing waves of the ocean. However it has been formed, it may contain a mix of rock types worn from the layers of a cliff or gathered by a river on its journey through a landscape.

OPENING SPREAD Kaikoura

PREVIOUS Gravel

OPPOSITE Melting snow assists with the formation of soils in alpine environments.

GRAVEL SOILS MAY BE LOCATED in alpine hillsides and valleys, along the sea shore or up riverbeds. In general they are found close to extremities with scarce plant life surviving in the cracks and crevices and hugging close to the earth. Gravel soils themselves are very low in the organic content off which plant life subsists, and the larger, generally harder, particles are hard for a root system to find its way through. The rock, though, does hold various minerals within it that will assist growth once a topsoil is developed.

Water retention is also a consideration – while movement of water through a soil is important, some absorption is ideal as it supports plant life through periods without rain.

We also need to take into account the surrounding climate when planning a garden in gravel soil. One of the reasons for a soil being low in organic matter is a lack of plant life. It should be remembered that it is plants themselves – along with insects and animals – that create organic matter. It is often the case that a heavy gravel soil is this way because the environment is hostile to life. Soil can also be an indicator of the history of a site, and the fact that there is no topsoil can relate to an absence of organic matter above ground.

Sparsely vegetated areas are often an indication of high winds, dryness and extremities of cold and heat, but within this environment you can look for clues as to where organic matter is naturally forming, and this will help you gather ideas for how your own soil can be modified. Often the surrounding environment is the first obstacle you need to overcome to establish your garden before you can look to the soil itself. It may be that shelter is required by creating walls or planting belts, or it may be that you

are best to look for the microclimates within a site where shelter is naturally formed to begin your garden and the development of soil.

The first growths that form in a gravelly environment are often mosses and lichens, closely followed by ground-hugging and small-leaved plants. These form in the cracks and crevices where water is collected and where nutrients from washed-in or blown-in organic matter will collect. It is in these formations that the secrets to transforming your soil lie. These low-lying plants in turn help to retain more organic matter.

Mosses retain water that plants will make use of, and act as a green mulch over an otherwise exposed and hostile environment. Small plants also help to catch organic matter and are in some ways self-sustaining. As leaves drop and decay, soil formation begins. The root systems of plants not only seek water and nutrients, they also create a structure which helps the formation of soil. Of course for all of this to occur, water is required. In an alpine environment plants often flourish in cycles that respond to the melting of snow; or, in a coastal or island environment, to rainy seasons. If you look at a natural landscape you can see how the patterns of water relate to the patterns the plants form across the landscape.

The problem with a rocky soil is that there is little organic

> In an alpine environment plants often flourish in cycles that respond to the melting of snow; or, in a coastal or island environment, to rainy seasons. If you look at a natural landscape you can see how the patterns of water relate to the patterns the plants form across the landscape.

matter to retain water when it is scarcer. You will need to either depend on plants that can withstand extended periods of dry, or find ways to retain water.

The landscape always has natural eddies and crevices where water collects or is directed. A rocky soil, while it does not retain moisture itself, can be utilised to channel water and hold collected organic matter in areas where you wish to begin vegetation.

The colours of a gravel soil can be as varied as the colours of rock itself. This will indicate the minerals within the rock, and give you an idea of the geological history of the area, but it won't change the basic method you will need to use to bring life to your garden. While nutrient in your soil is very important, it is easier to adjust once you have developed the correct structure in the soil for growing. Trying to add nutrients or minerals into a soil without organic matter is like pouring dye into an ocean. It will be quickly washed through and soon be untraceable.

Another variable to identify in stony soils is the softness of the stone. Limestone and sandstone are gravelly but can be crushed quite easily, while harder schists and basalts require machinery to break them apart. The softer stones will break down to some degree once you begin to develop good organic matter, so they tend to be more fertile if well managed than a harder stone. This is because as a plant's root systems form they are able to penetrate

> Trying to add nutrients or minerals into a soil without organic matter is like pouring dye into an ocean. It will be quickly washed through and soon be untraceable.

the soil with more ease. They are, though, easily compacted again if left exposed or driven over, which is ideal if you wish to inhibit plant growth in areas such as paths.

SOIL APPROACH

GRAVEL SOILS MAY BE A HOSTILE ENVIRONMENT in which to begin a garden, but they are a great example of how landscapes can be transformed from the most extreme moonscapes to abundance. We have a wealth of experience from farmers and gardeners across the globe and across the ages to learn from. What we need to understand is that the creation of soil is a process that gardening can be a part of; and a healthy garden creates good dirt.

There is a beautiful tale told in the *National Geographic* of African farmers working on the edge of the Saharan desert in an environment where droughts and intensive ploughing had left the soil harder than asphalt. In this rocky environment severe famines led farmers back to traditional methods, of which one of the most successful is called *cordons pierreux*. It is as simple as laying lines of stones across a field. These stones need only be as large as a fist, but they create a collection point where water, finer particles of silt and then seeds collect. This creates a band of vegetation, be it grasses or low-growing perennials and shrubs, which in turn creates organic matter. Whether you view these plants as weeds or desirable plants, it's important to understand that they're initiating the process of a living soil formation, much in the same way as we can use flax and manuka to restore forest in New Zealand. Water

is slowed and held in this band of vegetation, which can then be replaced by trees and shrubs. They in turn create shade and shelter, which both reduce water loss, and in time these stone deserts became productive and highly valuable land.

As well as using stone above the ground to change the environment, creating pits is another technique popular in Africa. Soil pits are dug into the heavy stone and filled with manure. This is then occupied and broken down by insects and microbial activity until the rainy season, when the farmers return to plant the holes. Here in New Zealand, as well as manure, a good available source of nutrients is dead possums which can either be buried deep beneath the planting or buried ready for a later planting. When planting over organic matter such as this, you will need to mound on top of it as the earth will subside as the matter decomposes. These methods remind me of my grandmother's vegetable garden. Her composting system involved digging a simple trench and burying the organic waste directly into this every day, pulling the soil over the top as she went. As she got to the end of a row she simply started another.

These simple stone rows are amazingly effective in precipitating life. There is no need, however, to stick to any particular line or pattern. It is the principle of using ridges and valleys that is key to success. For a natural garden, terracing with informal stone lines will

> My grandmother's composting system involved digging a simple trench and burying the organic waste directly into this every day, pulling the soil over the top as she went.

create a form to capture water, as well as the ability to add organic matter to speed up the process. When you are introducing compost, planting mix or topsoil to a site, you need to consider the base you are working on. A heavier topsoil is less likely to wash through a gravel base than a finer planting mix. This can be enhanced with compost as you plant, and then mulched heavily.

GARDEN PREPARATION

MULCHING IS APPROPRIATE FOR MOST SOIL TYPES. Not only does it reduce water loss (and weeds!), it becomes your future soil. Even with no added topsoil or compost, regular mulching will create a marked increase in the organic matter and therefore the quality of your soil.

Of course, one of the greatest challenges of a rocky soil is that it can be impenetrable. Taking a spade to it can be not only strenuous but dangerous – if you strike the rock you are likely to end up with jarring vibrations, if not a spade ricocheting back into your chin. So, if you can't go down, go up. Lifting your garden and your trees out of the ground can be achieved by mounding, terracing or having raised beds, depending on the site. The important details to remember are that plant roots need to be covered and that soil can be washed away. Mulching around roots is very important when mounding around trees, but be careful not to raise the soil level around the trunks where it can cause the stems to rot. You can use newspapers, straw, bark mulches or thin layers of lawn clippings. These help form the soil in more ways

than one. On the surface they begin to break down with the help of important bacteria, insects and fungi, which assists a plant's surface roots. In turn the plant pulls in organic matter as deep as its roots can go. Water follows the roots, as does air and all sorts of tiny organisms we are only just beginning to understand.

It is advisable to dig into the ground where you can, even if it is to create some cracks beneath where you plan to plant. These cracks will become areas where water and organic matter can slowly seep, weakening and softening the gravelly ground. It also creates weak points where the roots of plants can push through and deeper channels that will further improve the soil.

I always plant with some rich organic matter such as sheep pellets at the base of the hole. This stimulates microbial activity and fungus, which work to break away the structure of the ground beneath, releasing minerals and bringing the dead stone to life.

Good dirt is not dust – it's a living soup of life that thrives beneath our feet. For us to achieve an abundant garden above, we need this to be a healthy thriving colony of goodness. The layers we build up above the ground are like offerings to the lords of an underworld that we are only just beginning to get a glimpse into, but on which we are completely dependent for a healthy world above.

STRUCTURE

WATER IS ESSENTIAL TO ORGANIC MATTER, which in turn is essential in the formation of a fertile soil. Corralling water can assist in the development of trees. One method of doing this is to create

OPPOSITE, ABOVE LEFT
When building supports for
climbing plants you should
consider prevailing winds.

ABOVE RIGHT Hedges can
be used to create shelter
from coastal winds but
they should be kept low to
preserve sun.

BELOW LEFT Gravel paths
in a kitchen garden help
to retain water; concrete
paving increases heat and
water run-off, which is not
desirable.

BELOW RIGHT Stone is used
to lift garden beds, allowing
for the addition of organic
matter.

a stone circle around the base of the tree. If the tree is planted on a slope, the circle should be incomplete, with the open side of the circle facing up to the highest point. This works as a cup, collecting any water and debris that move down the slope. On the flat, a simple circle helps to reduce run-off and makes mulching where it is most needed easy and tidy. If you have planned a more formal layout for your garden, you can make use of stone walls and edges to create ridges behind which soil can develop. Paths, too, should be considered to help filter water through and into the soil. Essentially the form of your hardscape can be as effective in improving your soil as what you add into a garden, if done thoughtfully.

Stone is an obvious material to make use of if available. But other materials are abundantly available in different environments: stacks of seaweed thrown up on a stone beach; an old tree stump; or driftwood delivered after a storm. Old wood will bring life to any garden, but it needs water to initiate the process. In a clay garden the soil will quickly act as a wick and bring water to a fallen tree, but in a stony environment you may need to help it. Make sure you bury the wood so that it is in contact with the earth, and ideally stack earth behind it to create an ideal growing environment where the wood can surrender back into the ground over time.

As soil begins to form, your ability to grow and build on it improves exponentially. A soil's acidity or mineral content will naturally change as the organic balance comes into play. You will need to accept and understand that a limestone soil will always be less acidic by nature, and this will affect the preference of some acid-loving plants such as camellias or azaleas or the colours of hydrangeas, but it doesn't prevent you from having a flourishing garden.

PRODUCTIVE GARDENING

IF YOU HAVE A DESIRE TO GROW FOOD in your garden, more attention should be given to the mineral and nutrient content in your soil. One of the main benefits of home-grown food is its freshness and quality, but if the minerals that you require are not in the ground, they will not be present in your food. Quality composts and mixes are tested for proper ratios, and if you are adding these to a garden bed they will be introducing the appropriate requirements to your soil. If you are making your own compost, however, you should test your soils to make sure they are appropriate for the crops you want to grow and for your own nutrient needs. In gravel soils where there is an absence of natural topsoil, more leaching will occur. Raised beds can help this on a larger scale, but many gardeners want to work straight into the ground, especially for big crops such as pumpkin and corn. An appropriate method

Where there are no trees there is obviously less fall from above, which is why the cracks and crevices or valleys and ravines become so important: these are the points where the process of collection begins.

is a no-dig gardening technique popular with permaculture and organic gardeners. I've always thought that 'earth up' is a better term to describe this way of growing, and that a forest system is a good analogy of how the principles work. In a natural system organic matter is renewed by the layers of debris that are collected on the surface. In a forest this is plentiful – fallen fruits, bird and animal droppings, leaf litter, old decaying trees and fall from storms. An earth-up approach is a simple mimicry of this concept. Of course in a stony environment this natural process is less intense. Where there are no trees there is obviously less fall from above, which is why the cracks and crevices or valleys and ravines become so important: these are the points where the process of collection begins.

When the soil beneath is low in organic matter you need to ensure that you replace and renew what you take from the soil. This can be done through composting and continual mulching. Rather than leaving a soil open after harvest, it should be covered over with an appropriate mulch (see Mulches, page 208), This is because soil oxidises and loses its organic value when it is exposed to the air. Leaving soil exposed also increases water loss, and in a stony soil this is one of the greater challenges a gardener faces, even in periods of high rainfall.

One of the best tricks I've come across for mulching a vegetable garden is to use the paths as a stockpile for woodchip. Unlike a properly graded bark mulch, woodchip can cause problems if laid fresh or green (when the trees' sap is still live). Stored on a garden path, however, it can be given time to decompose. As this begins to occur, the path will form a soil layer and weeds will become more vigorous. The woodchip can then be shovelled onto the beds either side, and the paths replenished with fresh woodchip.

MATERIALS

BECAUSE GRAVEL SOILS ARE LOW in organic matter, the key to transformation is increasing the volume of living material on your site. Before fertiliser or trace elements are considered, your main focus should be building the body of this soil.

In terms of materials, mulches are of high value, be they bark mulches, straw, lawn clippings, leaf moulds or even newspapers. Ideally these materials should come from a local source that you can easily replenish, as the process of making soil is not a

one-hit wonder. Think in layers over time. All the wonderful rich soils that we enjoy are the result of thousands of years of organic cycles, so you should expect the process of growing your soil to be one where this resource will accumulate over time. The more your garden grows the more it will offer to this process and the less you need to bring from outside. At this point composts and sheep pellets become luxurious extras, enriching a developing soil with extra goodness.

When planting, using well-balanced compost and sheep pellets will encourage healthy organisms into the soil, which will help set things off to a good start.

Seaweed

Seaweed is a wonderful source of minerals, and if you live near a coast it can be harvested after a storm and processed to create liquid fertilisers or added to compost. Giant kelps are the hardest to process as they need to be chopped to be useful. This process can be expedited by laying the seaweed out to dry in the sun. First wash it down to remove the residual salt, and then, as it dries, it becomes brittle and papery and can be crushed or smashed into smaller pieces that are ideal for composting and soil conditioning.

Bones

Our soils need calcium in the same way we do, and bones are a wonderful reserve. Buried alone they are very stable and take a long time to break into the soil and release these reserves. Several

processes are used by gardeners to release this calcium so it is accessible. Blood and bone is ground bonemeal from the meat industry and has long been a traditional source of calcium for soils. Rudolf Steiner, most famous as an educationalist, developed a theory of 'biodynamics', which came about when farmers in his region asked him to assist with soils of decreasing quality. In 1929 he predicted that modern agriculture would cause the decline of the honeybee. Part of his approach to soil involves burying bones filled with manure as a way to create microbial infestation of the bone which releases some of the calcium. The other practice is to burn the bones; they can then be broken into smaller pieces suitable for conditioning soil and adding to compost.

Feathers, hair and orange peel

If you take the image of earth as all the colours of the rainbow into your practice of soil management, it will help you think more broadly about what you might put into your compost. While adding materials such as feathers from a chicken coop, or hair from a haircut, into the compost is not possible for all gardeners, these are examples of thinking outside the square when it comes to composting. Little things such as emptying the hair from your brush or the clippings from toenails will assist in adding trace elements to the soil. Don't just limit your composting to the obvious: if it doesn't have chemicals in it and is not plastic, throw it in. From children's art projects to old clothes, if it once was alive, chances are it can be composted.

OPPOSITE, ABOVE LEFT
Pseudopanax ferox with
Leucospermum

ABOVE RIGHT Native
Pachystegia

BELOW LEFT Thyme,
Pseudowintera and
Muehlenbeckia

BELOW RIGHT A fallen
tree creates shelter for
the garden and is host
to epiphytes.

PLANTING

LIKE THE AFRICAN FARMERS WHO STARTED with stone lines to initiate the formation of soil, we too need to plan our gardens in a way that will both retain and create organic matter. This is the key to a successful garden. When planning we need to consider the effects of erosion from water and wind, how shelter can be kept, and how water can be maximised on the site without the need for intensive irrigation that is dependent on external water.

For life to exist above, it is dependent on a community of life below the ground. Like our bodies – which are buzzing with microorganisms that keep our health in balance – plants, too, do not live independently. What occurs beneath the surface is as mystical as the stars above us. Recent studies have shown that webs of fungus grow between communities of plants, and electrical pulses are sent from one plant to another to warn of attacks by insects or grazing mammals; this results in a neighbouring tree releasing toxic defences into the leaves. New Zealand's great kauri forests are suffering a potential demise from a small microorganism invisible to our eyes. This shows the power of the smallest organisms to affect the most mighty. A gravel soil has structure, but is low in the organic matter that hosts this underworld. To bring fertility into this environment we need to introduce the decomposing matter that becomes soil.

Even when taking the most natural of approaches to creating a garden, we still require spaces to sit, paths to walk on, and vegetable gardens; and we need to consider views and the sun as well as shelter. By manipulating the environment above the ground we

OPPOSITE Soil forms in
crevices in a cliff face,
allowing plants to grow.

can create microclimates that will affect the soil beneath.

The best advice I can give a gardener who is starting on an
exposed site is to think of the garden as having generations. Your
garden is going to change, and as it changes the aspect and plants
you are able to grow will change with it. A rocky environment is
normally so because it is exposed to the elements, whether it is the
sea, an icy wind or the desert sun. When you're trying to modify
this landscape, shelter is
the first part of the process.
With shelterbelts, though,
I recommend you think
of them in layers rather
than the traditional fast-
growing hedgerows. A
shelterbelt should have
a mix of at least five species that serve different roles through
different cycles of time, and offer support to each other as they
develop. This avoids the cycle which many are faced with of a
shelterbelt reaching a point of old age where it needs to be replaced
but its removal will expose the house or garden to the elements
again. A shelterbelt is not just changing the environment above the
ground; its shade slows water loss and reduces the oxidisation that
occurs when a soil is constantly exposed to the sun.

A community of plants has a root system beneath that is
getting to work underground. A border planting changes the flow
of water and nutrients in the surrounding area. Planting more than
one species makes this network stronger beneath the ground as
well as above.

> A shelterbelt should have a mix of at least five species that serve different roles through different cycles of time, and offer support to each other as they develop.

A boundary planting can be as formal or informal as desired, but planting in communities will increase its success both short- and long-term. Your plant communities should include a mix of slow-growing trees to provide your ultimate upper structure, fast-growing trees or medium shrubs that may be short-lived but that will give results while your upper storey develops, and understorey plants such as grasses and flaxes that will stabilise the ground. Rather than thinking of shelter on a single plane, think of it in terms of transition over time. Rather than requiring one plant to cover an area, think of a mosaic that works on a range of heights, through different periods, both above and below the ground.

When establishing these shelterbelts along legal boundaries or for protection from prevailing winds, it's good to think about how water is flowing through the soil beneath. There may be areas where shelter is not required and perhaps maintaining views is of importance, but it is good to give thought to creating mixed communities or bands of planting that will effectively slow water movement on your site. Think of the roots below as creating dams to collect both organic matter and water. This is a very valuable technique with which to grow soil.

GARDENS IN GRAVEL SOILS

WHILE NEW ZEALAND IS RICH IN TOPSOIL, other parts of the world that have been intensively farmed by humans for many centuries are much lower in organic matter. Their landscapes have suffered years of erosion and intensive farming, and the soils are typically poor in comparison to ours. Stony gravel soils are common in a Mediterranean landscape, and gardeners there are used to working in a gravel landscape where topsoil is at a premium. One solution is intensive irrigation and a reforming of the landscape into lawns and swimming pools; however, contemporary designers are rejecting this approach. Not only is it not sustainable as pressures on the landscape increase, it creates blobs of bright green lawns around mansions that stand out like scars on an otherwise muted and ethereal landscape. The lawns and gardens are trampling on the view and the natural beauty (however manmade that natural state may be) to a point where they might as well be plastic, such is their disconnect to the landscape.

Stony gravel soils are common in a Mediterranean landscape, and gardeners there are used to working in a gravel landscape where topsoil is at a premium.

It is of course difficult as a landscape designer to convince a client that what you wish them to do with a landscape is nothing at all. It also takes a very humble designer to suggest that the beauty that is there in natural form is perhaps greater than anything we can imagine. Within this landscape, a range of styles that are both drawn from or blend into the existing vista have become the norm.

In Greece, Thomas Doxiadis has taken an approach of designing gardens that unravel into the landscape. Gardens planted close to a house are tightly and minimally planted in careful and controlled drifts. Deliberate blocks are placed to frame views, soften the architecture into the landscape, and create spaces which are both beautiful and functional. At this point his designs, although wonderfully executed, follow the rules that most of us would when we lay out a garden. But as the garden moves away from the house and into the landscape, the planting patterns change. The spacing between plants becomes further apart, until at the fringes of the landscape the planting is sparse. Rather than defining the boundaries of a garden, instead it gradually dissolves into the scape beyond. Like a water-colourist's brush melting a horizon into the sky to indicate a point we know exceeds our vision, the garden does not at any point begin or end.

In other projects Doxiadis has used the patterns of the natural landscape to break it into productive zones. Because of the low organic matter remnant in these soils – which have been part of the cultural landscape for thousands of years – there is no luxury of dividing an area into convenient squares. The low valleys are utilised in the form that the land takes, as this is where the water is naturally captured. Terracing that follows the lines and natural forms of the landscape allows further productivity, carefully capturing and directing available water most effectively.

While areas close to the house, especially those for vegetables, may require some irrigation, the existing plants of the wider landscape have already proven their ability to handle the ebb and flow of the seasons. With richer soils and a more abundant landscape such lines are not as definitive unless marked by fencing, but where resources are scarce the line between the irrigated landscape and that beyond is graphic.

In gravelly areas of New Zealand, such as Kaikoura or the hills of Wanaka, gardeners need to think carefully about how to blend their own mark with the views beyond. Gardening that requires the least redistribution of resources is the most sustainable – and attainable.

This does not mean there is no place for the manmade and for our own folly: a garden, after all, is a relationship with the land. But understanding the landscape from the soil beneath to the winds above and working in sync with it gives the dancer a sweeter step.

LESSONS FROM NATURE

BRITISH GARDEN DESIGNER JAMES BASSON runs his landscape design practice in the South of France with his wife, Helen Basson. Their approach is not dissimilar to Doxiadis's, in its intention to draw the outside landscape seamlessly into the garden. Their gardens are also created in gravel soils, and in an environment that has to contend not only with wind, snow and high summer temperatures, but the increasing blights of fire that the Mediterranean is facing. Basson's work is taken from observation of the natural patterns on the surrounding hillsides. There are no lawns with two or three varieties of American rye or English fescues. Instead, areas of turf are replaced with mixes of up to 30 or so species a square metre of ground-hugging perennials that have proven themselves able to handle the infertile stone soils and extremities of climate. Traditional lawns require a high water input and constant grooming, which is not practical or sustainable in an arid, stony environment. These mosaic lawns serve the same purpose and allow species to compete as the garden goes through different cycles of time and seasonal shifts.

The architecture of the gardens, too, is carefully crafted to provide functionality of spaces for comfortable living, as well as directing water to key areas of the garden. Basson's work involves hours of observation of where plants naturally occur and the complexities of the communities that they form. Old Roman roads running above the surrounding pasture create bands of growth along the edges where water is directed. In old quarries the process of revegetation follows the lines of cracks and crevices. Rather

than curse the stony soil and try to impose a new regime onto the landscape, Basson's work instead shows a love and understanding of the role of rock in creating shelter for a plant community. Rock and gravel take many forms, both natural and crafted, to create walls and terraces that capture water and provide shelter and shade. He creates stunning gardens that are as habitable for us as the plants that occupy them. Despite Basson's work being primarily gardens of privilege, the basis for these methods is not at all dissimilar to the *cordons pierreux* of the African farmers working on the edge of the Saharan desert.

As well as using stone from the site to trace water and its path and to assist the accumulation of organic matter, Basson has also explored creating gardens from seed. His garden, 'Peille', is a very successful example of this. Basson grew all of the plants initially from seed. He then divided and propagated the successful plants to fatten the garden. This came from a frustration of watching the fat, plump greenhouse plants fail after a year or two in the field, while out on the hills lavenders and the like of the same species grew for decades without hindrance.

In New Zealand, designers such as Philip Smith are known for their work within the patterns of an alpine landscape, making use of stone and contours to create gardens that wind through natural patterns rather than being imposed on the landscape. These contemporary gardens use natural outcrops of rocks to create informal terraces, restoring native plants to the landscape from which they were previously cleared for farming. This process of revegetation is, in the course of human history, a more recent concept and is currently most common in areas of New Zealand, the Americas and Australia. It is the most effective way of rebuilding soil. As areas of Europe face rising temperatures and fire risk, it is possible that a process of revegetation could be used to both cool and restore soils that have long been poor and

FOLLOWING SPREAD Rock
shelves on a bank help to
stabilise soil and create
crevices for planting.

unproductive. In the past revegetation tended to happen as a
course of abandonment as soils became less fertile, but as cities
and towns fill more of these gaps a more deliberate process of
wilding may need to be considered to ensure future soil reserves.

SOIL AND CULTURE

LANDSCAPE ARCHITECT DIANA WIESNER WORKS in Bogotā
in her homeland of Colombia. The city is a very intense urban
environment which, due to poverty, was developed with little
green space. Wiesner's work sits mostly in the public realm, but is
focused on reigniting a connection with the beautiful mountainous
landscape that sits around the concrete towers. As well as designing
parks, she has set out to create an engagement with the hills – where
once people lived, grew food and gathered from the forests – using
dance, music and old traditions. So in the hills they now have
concerts and festivals and art exhibitions, as well as planting days
and gardening workshops. Her work is a reminder to me that the
soil we seek is part of our culture. The ancient soil reserves of the
Amazon that we look to replicate are part of a human ecology; they
would not have occurred without us. The ingredients to create good
soil do not need to be gathered from far and distant continents;
instead, a growing soil which will allow us to produce whatever
we require comes from our waste and refuse. In cooking, eating,
drinking, building homes, heating, making pottery, we create the
ingredients for healthy soil. An abundant life returned to the ground
provides for future generations.

INGREDIENTS GUIDE

ROCK

Can be positioned beneath and above the ground to control the flow of water and therefore the accumulation of organic matter within a soil.

LAWN CLIPPINGS

Lawns need regular cutting, which removes large amounts of nitrogen from a garden. This has a high value when renewing soils, but should be applied in thin layers.

HEDGE TRIMMINGS

These can be used as an immediate mulch over woody areas of a garden. The thicker the trunk of the tree, the thicker the stem of the hedge you can use.

MULCH

The woodier the plant, the woodier the mulch is a good rule of thumb. All open earth should be covered over to maintain its health.

BIOCHAR

Charcoal not only creates a stable soil condition, it also stores organic matter cleared from above in the soil, so has value as a way of sequestering carbon that would otherwise be released atmospherically.

SEAWEED

If you dry and crumble seaweed it is easy to mix it through soils or compost. It is rich in minerals and adds nutritional value as well as organic matter. In dry areas seaweed is best rinsed to reduce salt.

COMPOST

Compost-like food is as good as its ingredients. If buying compost, look on the back of the bag and see if it has been tested and if it contains trace elements. If making your own, remember that it's part of a cycle, and the more care you take with your compost the better the quality.

WOOD

Can be used to raise gravel soils where they are difficult to dig into. It can also be layered with soil to help water retention and to reduce leaching of topsoil as it develops.

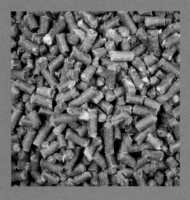

SHEEP PELLETS

Chicken, cow and sheep manure all have high value in the growth of soil because of their microbial content as well as nutrient levels. The wool content of sheep pellets also helps soil structure and aeration.

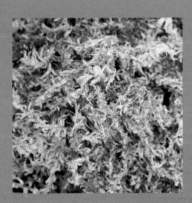

SPHAGNUM MOSS

Can be used as a mulch or in ground.

LEAF MULCH

Leaves can be collected and allowed to compost on new beds or used to create leaf mould to mulch beds in spring and autumn.

PLANTING APPROACH

Use stone to help the formation and collection of soil in the landscape. Stone can be used to raise gardens, build terraces or create simple circles around trees.

Add shelter using walls or planting to create microclimates. Consider the direction of sun in winter and summer, as well as prevailing winds.

Observe the flow of water through the landscape and lay out gardens to capture it. Capture water on roofs to store, and design sloped paths so water is redirected to gardens.

Grow small plants or plants from seed that will form deep root structures, helping to support the plant through dry periods.

Modified soils

In this modern world where the natural landscape is becoming increasingly altered, there is a greater need for manmade soils. Whether it's for containers or to create roof or urban gardens, the soils required need to be appropriate for these different circumstances. When we garden in the ground we are connected to an ecology which extends beyond the boundaries of our fencelines. The rain that falls into our gardens is part of a larger system, and so is all the life in our soil. Worms do not care which side of the fence you are on.

IF THE SITUATION IS RIGHT, worms will appear as if from nowhere. But on a rooftop or in a container on a deck we don't have the benefit of this bigger system, so we need to create a healthy garden within the limitations of our space. This means thinking about drainage, fertiliser and water retention. In some situations your containers might not be that far removed from your main gardens and you can benefit from any compost and worm juice that are produced; but in intensive city environments where containers are your only garden, you will need to start from scratch.

There are many situations where you may introduce a soil medium to a site. In most urban and suburban situations this is likely to involve adding composts to vegetable beds, building new gardens, reshaping areas within a space, or restoring soil after a period of construction onsite. In all of these situations you are likely to need to purchase soils, and it is important to understand the purpose of different mixes and their appropriate applications.

TOPSOIL VERSUS FILL

THERE ARE TWO MAIN TYPES of basic soil you can buy: topsoil and fill. Fill can be anything and may not even be consistent. It can include crushed concrete and stone, and is often specified by an engineer to ensure a site is stable; but it is not necessarily going to be great for your garden. Fill can vary greatly in quality, and so is not something you should just order over the phone unless quality is of no concern.

Topsoil should be a loam – which is a mix of sand, silt, clay

OPPOSITE ABOVE Plants in planters require more water than plants in a garden. Choosing suitable plants can help avoid dependence on irrigation.

OPPOSITE BELOW If you have sandy or low-nutrient soils, containers can allow you to grow a broader range of plants in richer mixes.

and organic matter – and you should find out what type of loam it is (clay, silt or sand) to be sure that it is appropriate for the garden that you are wanting to create. The other question to ask is whether the topsoil is sterilised or screened. A sterilised soil will be weed-free but it will also be free of all other life, so this is only suitable as a base and will need to be supplemented with a mix with some organic content, such as compost or a layer of planting mix. Screened mix is graded, which means it is shaken through a mesh to ensure rocks and other rubble are removed from the mix. Screened soil does not mean it is weed-free, as seeds cannot be removed through this process.

SOIL APPROACH

BEFORE YOU SELECT A MIX for the garden you are creating, you need to understand its limitations. The first thing to consider is drainage. If the water can't escape from the container or area you are trying to plant, you run the risk of stagnation, which is a breeding ground for root diseases. Only plants that are adapted to growing in flood zones can cope with extended periods of being submerged; many plants drown and then decompose as the different microbes that thrive in these swampy conditions take over. If there is no way of draining water you need to create a cavity in the base using a depth of scoria. This depth will vary depending on the size of your container, but if you fill 10 to 20 per cent it should be sufficient. You will also need to consider the root systems of the plants you are planting. The roots will be limited

by a container's size and this will limit the growth above. In some
situations this is desirable, but if you have planted a pohutakawa
tree in a concrete planter, for example, it is likely that at some
point its roots will slowly and gently force the pot apart as they
seek new nutrients.

Drainage is essential in contained soil environments. If water
cannot escape, the environment will become anaerobic and you
will have problems related to this, such as soil diseases. This is
one of the reasons most potting mixes, like a good loam, have
some sand content. To assist drainage, one of the old tricks
used by gardeners is to fill the base of the pot with broken old
terracotta pots and crockery. I always put broken crockery or
pottery in my compost bin. The main reason is that I know it does
more good there than it would in a landfill; but I also like the idea
that I'm contributing to an archaeological layer of history. In
hundreds of years old Japanese Imari porcelain, English china
and local earthenware may be found there.

FERTILISERS

SLOW-RELEASE FERTILISERS ARE IMPORTANT IN POTS, where
the soil-to-root ratio is much less than in ground-grown plants.
For plants to thrive they need a more intense supply of nutrients.
Slow-release fertilisers vary in the way they release nutrients.
The most basic types release them continuously over a three-
month period. This release starts when it is put into a soil mix;
so if you leave those bags of potting mix sitting in the shed the

fertiliser will be releasing into the mix as it waits to be used. The nutrients are still in the bag, but you've lost the advantage of giving your plants a slow and even food source. I tend to use any mix that has been sitting around for extended periods to mulch under trees and shrubs and use fresh potting mix for the garden.

While a three-month release is normally the cheapest slow-release fertiliser, there are others that work in a more sophisticated way and these are more reliable. The best often have three different-coloured granules (you will quite often see the different colours in a mix) each with a different period of release. This means your mix has enough nutrients to keep plants going for extended periods. You should always check a mix to see how long it is going to last, and make note of this in a garden diary.

While these slow-releases are excellent and keep the potting mix going well, I like to supplement plants with a liquid fish fertiliser. This maintains microbial activity in the soil. A good potting mix comes with plenty of organic matter, but an injection of fish fertiliser helps to create a healthy buzz of bacteria. Worm juice, too, keeps the microbial activity high, which is especially hard to get going in containers.

A good mix comes with plenty of organic matter, but an injection of fish fertiliser helps to create a healthy buzz of bacteria. Worm juice, too, keeps the microbial activity high, which is especially hard to get going in containers.

ORGANIC CONTENT

WE CAN LEARN A LOT FROM CONTAINER MIXES about how quickly the organic content is transformed from soil, or brown carbon, into the living plant, or green carbon. Pull out a potted tomato at the end of a summer's growth and the volume of soil left has greatly reduced – sometimes by more than half. This is why we need to keep replenishing our food gardens, even more so than other gardens. Many vegetables are annuals, and every time we harvest and replant we are taking out a volume of the organic content from the soil. Much of this can be composted but, unless we have a composting toilet to recapture the nutrients we've processed, much of it is leaving the system in the energy we expend during the day.

This is why planting mixes are designed to be heavier in content than potting mix. When filling raised beds with mix you want to avoid subsidence, which is more likely to occur the greater the organic content of the mix. Organic content comes from many different sources – normally from agricultural waste such as forestry bark, mushroom compost, which is full of beneficial fungi, coconut fibre, sheep manure or dags, and, in some cases, manure from zoos or even human sewage. While the idea of composting our own waste is not for everyone, it once was commonplace. In England centuries ago the waste from the wealthy received a higher price in the marketplace as their diet was considered richer and more nutrient-loaded.

WATER RETENTION AND DISTRIBUTION

THE OTHER QUALITY TO LOOK FOR in a potting mix is how water is held and distributed. Experienced gardeners will have noticed how rain will simply not penetrate a pot that has not been watered and in which the soil is root-bound. Quality potting mixes are designed to distribute the water evenly throughout. Water crystals, which expand to retain water, were once popular,

but these have now largely been replaced by wetting agents.
These work in the same way as soap works, separating oils that
help with the penetration of the water down into the root zone.
It then reaches a point of saturation where sand particles in the
mix allow excess water to drain away.

MATERIALS

THERE IS A MULTITUDE OF MIXES available on the market. It's
not just about choosing a reliable brand, but understanding the
difference between the products out there. Compost is the most
common mix to be misused. To the inexperienced gardener it just
looks like good smelly dirt, and the assumption can be that you
can't have too much of a good thing – but you can. Compost is a
soil conditioner used to enrich an existing soil, while other mixes
are designed to plant directly into. Different plants have different
needs. Some, such as orchids, need a very loose mix of bark or
charcoal. Some, like bulbs, prefer a drier mix as too much water
can cause rot. It's important to get the mix of ingredients right,
whether you are making it yourself or buying a ready-made mix.

Planting mix

A planting mix should be close to the texture of a good loam. It
should hold together when wet and squeezed together in a ball, but
fall apart easily if you shake it. It has a lower organic content than
compost, so it can be planted directly into. It is more fertile than
a topsoil and will subside over time. With all soil that is moved
around there is some 'fluffage' that occurs. A clay soil increases its
volume even as it is excavated, as the particles are separated by
air. This means if you are excavating a volume of soil you need to

add 30 per cent to allow for the number of bins or trucks that will be taking it away. By the same token any new soil, whatever the quality, will compact over time. Most landscapers water the soil to help reduce this, as watering helps the soil settle and reduces the air content or fluffage. Another trick is to mound up the soil. For example, if you are laying a flat lawn, creating a soft mound through the middle of the lawn will counter the natural settling, and instead of a dip it will settle to flat over time. This overfilling can also be done in planters and new garden beds. It's not a bad sign if your soil levels drop, because it's an indication of good organic quality. If you are filling very deep garden beds it pays to layer the soil, especially if your subsoil is very poor. A high-quality mix on top of a compacted subsoil can become similar to a sealed planter with very low permeability. This can cause problems with the root systems and reduce soil health. It is therefore advisable to put in a median layer of loam or topsoil with a final depth of planting mix above. Good soil relates to the flow of water and creating an even distribution through your soil. When a soil structure has been damaged, we need to try and recreate it to some extent, so creating an artificial stratum is best practice.

Planting mix does not generally have a slow-release fertiliser mixed into it, but it is fertile and ready to grow. You can add sheep pellets (always my favourite) or the fertiliser that best suits the requirements of your particular garden.

Container mix

Container mix or potting mix are both mixes for growing in pots and containers and are interchangeable. There are many different mixes on the market and it's hard to know the difference between them, other than the price, but generally the difference is in the quality of the ingredients. More expensive mixes have fertilisers that will slowly release to your plants over a period of up to 18 months. High-end mixes have more specialised ingredients such as coco fibre to help with water retention. They include wetting agents that distribute water through a mix evenly. If you are buying one of these mixes you shouldn't be adding anything to your plants, unless you want to give them a seaweed fertiliser to keep the microorganisms buzzing.

Specialty mixes

Specialty mixes are, as the name suggests, put together for a particular purpose or need. Orchid mix, for example, is primarily bark with a small amount of organic matter. Many commonly grown orchids are epiphytic or grow in infertile alpine soils; so are better receiving nutrients in the form of liquid seaweed fertiliser than in compost. Compost can burn or rot the roots, which are capable of absorbing moisture directly from the atmosphere. In comparison a cactus or succulent mix has a very high sand content, which is free-draining and yet fine. Many nurseries work with potting mix companies to design their own mixes that are best suited to the plants they grow. Some natives, for example, benefit from a mix with a clay content; while edible plants need good organic matter and key trace elements.

Seed-raising mix

Seed-raising mix is designed to create the ideal environment for seed germination. Every little seed has within it all that it needs, apart

OPPOSITE Andrew Wilson and Cavin Macdonald's award-winning roof garden for the Singapore Garden Festival required special engineering to ensure the soil medium could sustain the plants and comply with weight restrictions.

from water and warmth, to develop its first roots and leaves. Anyone who has grown sprouts at home will be familiar with how these magic parcels open and grow when the conditions are just right. In a seed mix you don't want high levels of nutrients, as spare nutrients will be taken up by moss or algae. Your seeds have the nutrients they need, and just require a good soil with low nutrients to assist them as they develop roots and true leaves. Drainage is of most importance so a good seed mix should have a higher sand content than other mixes. Too much water can rot seeds. Seeds of large native trees such as karaka and puriri just need to be placed on top of a mix. Smaller seeds tend to like to be buried with a thin scattering of earth, as would accumulate over them naturally in a season.

Pumice sand

When people talk about sand in garden mixes, or sand to start cuttings in, be warned it's not the same as the sand you find at your local beach. Sand from the beach or ocean floor is likely to have a salt content, which is not good for your plants. Some builders' mix sand is dredged and can often contain salts.

The different types of pumice sands are soft and coarse. Coarse sands are better for horticulture. The other difference is that the screening sands that you purchase specifically for growing are sterilised and tested to make sure they don't have a lime content. This is especially important when you are growing from cuttings that have essentially an open wound. The reason we start cuttings in sand is to keep the water from sitting around the stem, where it tends to rot out rather than root out!

OPPOSITE Mixes can be customised to meet the needs of different plant varieties.

Commercial compost

While homemade compost is an important part of looking after our soils and reusing waste, buying compost to nourish the soil when you plant is an excellent way to grow topsoil and improve soil conditions. There are lots of different composts on the market, but they are not equal. The best composts have trace elements as well as good organic content. You should also look for products that are batch-tested – this means the manufacturer monitors each batch of compost, checking for growth of soil organisms or weeds as well as ensuring that the balance of trace element nutrients is ideal.

Compost is probably the mix that confuses most new gardeners. It is best to think of it as a soil conditioner rather than a planting medium, and be aware that planting directly into it can burn young plants or new roots. Think of it as the cream on top of milk – a little on the surface is a good thing, but too much and your body won't thank you later. No garden should be without it, but nor do we want to drown a garden in it. A thin layer across the surface of new beds, dug through as you plant and then mulched over the top, or some mixed into the soil around a new tree, will get your garden off to a great start. If your soil is already vital and has plenty of worms, they will mix the compost through for you, ensuring it is spread down into the root system of your plant. Alongside this beneficial fungi will follow, supporting the health of all the plants in your garden.

Coconut fibre

Coco fibre is a common and valuable ingredient in many mixes. It has excellent water-retention quality and works like a sponge. It is used in potting mixes, and as liners in hanging baskets. It has the advantage of being very light, which makes it easy to work with and appropriate where weight may be an issue. Coconut fibre

OPPOSITE ABOVE Cacti need mixes with a higher sand content.

OPPOSITE BELOW Lawns need mixes with a lower organic content so they don't subside as the organic matter breaks down.

has similar qualities to peat, a soil which is very rich in organic matter compared to the other particles; however while peat is very valuable, it is not replaceable, so it is not good practice to use peat-based mixes. Coconut fibre is a far more sustainable material.

Lawn mix

Lawns can be wonderful things. As pressure on space reaches a premium in urban centres, our lawns are being challenged, and rightly so. In a small space we should look at all our options and utilise our land to the full. But lawns aren't all bad. Cricket, croquet, picnics and handstands are all best on a nice stretch of grass. Grasses are also wonderful for soil and worms. While they might not look like much on top, the roots of grasses grow deep into the earth, creating reserves of carbon. Worms love a good lawn, as long as it's not too well tended with chemicals and the like, and in a healthy worm-filled earth your soil will grow for you. For lawn-lovers one of the main challenges (ignoring the weeds) is creating the perfect free-draining, level ground. Too much organic matter in a lawn soil causes subsidence. Not enough drainage and the water-hungry grasses will be sitting in a bog. A lawn will do well in any loam soil, and a good lawn mix has some weight to it. Make sure, if you use topsoils, that they are sterilised or you will be battling the weeds. The healthiest lawn soil is that of the carefree gardener who is happy to let the daisies and dandelions share the space. What could be better than daisy-chains and dandelion tea!

Sphagnum moss

Sphagnum moss is a natural material that grows on the West Coast of New Zealand and is sustainably harvested under guidelines laid out by the Department of Conservation to ensure the overall moss reserves are not depleted. Sphagnum is harvested using pitchforks rather than machinery to prevent peripheral damage to the sites. In New Zealand we have lost large areas of peatland where sphagnum grows, so there is provision in place to make sure remaining reserves are well cared for. Commercially it is sold both dry and live, and is commonly used in hanging baskets to line the outside and help retain water. It is also popular in floristry to extend the life of cut flowers.

Mulches

Mulches are invaluable for the growth of healthy soil. Ideally they can be applied in both spring and autumn, or between crops in the vegetable garden. The best mulch to use depends on where in your garden you are using it. My rule of thumb is the woodier the plant, the woodier the mulch can be. Annual plants like vegetables are turning over the soil quickly, so a soft mulch like pea straw is ideal. Bark mulches are wonderful for most garden beds and borders as the growth is slower, and a heavier mulch helps to supress weeds while still feeding the soil. When you put mulch down, spreading a layer of compost or blood and bone first will further help to enrich the soil. Always feed before mulching, rather than leaving sheep pellets or composts exposed to the light. Compost and sheep pellets are loaded with healthy bacteria and fungi that live in soils and are best buried in.

FEEDING THE SOIL

TRACE ELEMENTS ARE ESSENTIAL FOR A HEALTHY GARDEN especially when producing your own food. Kay Baxter is one of our leading organic gardeners and is most respected for her years spent gathering a national collection of heirloom fruit trees, vegetables and berries among other treasures. The Koanga Institute is one of New Zealand's treasures. Koanga holds the largest collection of organically certified heritage fruit trees and seed in New Zealand. It also offers courses on organic and nutrient-rich food production. Baxter changed her approach to gardening after many years of organic gardening when she discovered that her produce was deficient in certain important nutrients compared to other produce. She had spent years gardening and working the land without chemicals to do the best for herself and her family, but her soil was missing key elements needed for health. Her new project has built on Koanga's wonderful collection of heirloom trees and plants to focus on nutrient-rich soil. You cannot have nutrient-dense food with a deficiency in the soil, however good the quality of your plant stock and growing conditions are. Most fertilisers focus on a few key elements, while Baxter states there are 48 different elements needed for healthy plant growth. She does this through creative composting – think diversity and imagination with all the colours of the rainbow. If you are making your own compost to grow food, then expect to put work into it. Being organic is not best practice if you only take care of what you leave *out* of your gardens. To get the value out of an organic garden you need to ensure that it is also a balanced and healthy garden. Make sure, if you are buying an organic mix, that it has been formulated to have the correct balance of nutrients and trace elements.

The right ingredients

All good compost recipes have the same basic ingredients: a good balance of greens and browns. Greens are the fresh organic matter that still has a high water content, such as weeds, lawn clippings, kitchen waste and manure (which I include here despite its colour). Greens include rotting fruit, flowers and other fresh

PREVIOUS LEFT New garden beds should be planted using planting mixes. Compost should not be used to fill new beds as it is too rich and can burn the roots of plants.

PREVIOUS RIGHT Aquatic plants need a mix of clay and sand. Too much organic matter can cause clouded water or increases of algae.

OPPOSITE This garden by designer Gary Marshall is a good example of mixed plant communities that support a healthy soil.

matter, so don't get too hung-up on the colour – think more about 'green' meaning fresh. Browns are dry waste, such as woody material, paper and leaves. These help keep air in the soil and are the equivalent of carbohydrates in our diet. Conditioners such as biochar can also be included as a layer of brown in your soil.

But *excellent* compost needs to have more than just these basic elements. Gary Marshall was a founder of the Auckland Permaculture Workshop and has recently set up a new collective called Resilio, which offers food-based gardens alongside architecture and other sustainable design

> Working with other gardeners in your neighbourhood gives you the opportunity to trade knowledge and experience.

practices. The main difference in Resilio's approach compared to other similar organisations is the currency in which they trade and the networks they have created. As well as being able to purchase a design in a conventional manner, the realisation of your garden can be paid for by joining the collective and contributing to establishing other people's gardens as well as your own. What you gain from this is not just a labour exchange but the experience of the people you are working alongside. Anyone who has tried to learn how to prune a fruit tree from a book will appreciate that hands-on practice with an experienced group is the best approach. Resilio also has the advantage of sharing local knowledge across age groups. These same values work for soil management. Within broad groups, local soils have their own characteristics and peculiarities. Working with other gardeners in your neighbourhood

gives you the opportunity to trade knowledge and experience.

Marshall advises you should always start with a soil test so you know what you are working with. He suggests the use of paramagnetic rock dust as a general addition of trace elements. The rock dust contains small doses of a large range of minerals – calcium, magnesium, phosphorous, potassium, sulphur, sodium, aluminium, silicon, chlorine, titanium, vanadium, chromium, manganese, iron, nickel, copper, zinc and strontium. For the rest it's all about using local resources. Marshall focuses on gathering biomass from around your community, such as leaves from the park and hedge prunings from neighbours' hedges, to build diversity that might be lacking in your own yard.

Chickens

For manure in a suburban setting the most accessible source is chooks. Chooks have lived alongside humans for thousands of years, and are effective urban manure machines. Fresh chicken manure is rich and very high in nitrogen, so normally it is best added to a composting system. It's not just the manure that has value to soil but the urine, too, has high levels of nitrogen. This is why laying mulch or straw through a chicken run is useful. This could be a bark mulch, straw, hedge trimmings, leaf drop or even newspaper. This brown carbon absorbs the nutrients from both the urine and manure, but also creates a habitat for insects. This encourages the chickens to forage through it, mixing the manure and mulch together. This mix can then be collected and laid on garden beds. Fresh manure alone can be laid out on resting beds to break down over winter months. It's still advisable to cover with a mulch to protect the soil over the winter months. Ideally chooks should be moved around or allowed to range freely, distributing manure evenly. This is not always possible where space is restricted and crops may be at risk, however; so in these circumstances, to get the benefits of the manure and keep their runs healthy, we need to redistribute it.

Hot-composting

Hot-composting is when you reserve your ingredients and create a layered square-metre block that all composts at the same time, rather than layering your compost as you go. This means the compost reaches higher temperatures, which is great if you want to compost weeds on-site. The process is not that different from normal composting, layering browns and greens, but with a higher ratio of browns. A good mix is 10 browns to 1 green, or even 30 browns to 1 green, and ideally a third of it is additional high-value waste such as manure and mineral-rich seaweed. Always add some old compost to ensure it's full of microorganisms. The pile is then compacted (make sure you chop everything up to help with this process) by jumping on top of it and watering. It's then left for a couple of months until mature. When it's done you can tell because it looks like good living compost!

Weeds like *Tradescantia* (or spiderwort) and *convolvulus* can also be cooked by laying them out on black plastic in the sun until they go to mush, and then adding them to your compost system.

Compost as you go

The most common approach to composting is the lasagne technique. This is when you layer greens over browns at a ratio of

1:2 with a sprinkling of lime and occasionally other goodies. If you get fruitflies, it's too acidic and you've forgotten the lime. As you normally collect larger amounts of browns, you can keep a pile next to your bins to load on top of the greens as you add kitchen waste or lawn clippings. Ideally you should keep a couple of bins on the go so you can have one resting while you build the other. You know your compost is healthy when it's writhing with worms. You can also add soil to your compost if it seems too rich, and then lots of browns with air between to stop the compost going sludgy.

The main challenge with compost is getting the balance right for your situation, as everyone's garden produces a different selection of waste. If you have too much green waste, a bokashi (see page 221) or a worm farm may be more appropriate. If you have too much brown waste, consider using some for mulch.

Leaf mould

Leaf mould is very popular where you have many deciduous trees: a pile of well-decomposed leaves are collected in autumn and reapplied to the garden in spring as a mulch. They can be laid thickly over areas of lawn to be prepared as gardens in the following season: make the layers 300–600mm deep. Dampen the piles so they don't blow away; or let the leaves compost for a while in a boxed bin before spreading on the new garden area.

Biodynamics

As mentioned earlier, Rudolf Steiner started the method of gardening called biodynamics, which is practised by many organic gardeners and those interested in permaculture. While some of Steiner's methods – such as mixing hair and dung in the horn of a cow and burying it in the soil – may sound like witchcraft, it's

important to consider the science behind his thinking. It makes
sense when you understand what is happening on a microbial
level in the soil and the need for a diverse range of nutrients for
ideal health. Microbes and fungi are key in releasing minerals
such as calcium from a solid form into small particles that can be
absorbed by root stuctures. All in all, biodynamics is in line with
modern thinking about soils. To grow food we need soil that is alive
and self-sustaining. To create soil that is alive we need a diverse
biomass full of bacteria and fungi and organic matter in all the
colours of the rainbow.

Fungi

If you have ever seen timelapse photography of how fungi grow you
will be able to visualise the complex web of fine threads that are
part of these amazing life forms. An old rotting log pulled apart is
often threaded with these white fibres, deconstructing the wood
into a form that is accessible to plants. These fibres are able to
penetrate into wood, stone and bone in a way not much else can.

My husband and I had an ancient cabbage tree in our garden
that was very elegant. I loved it despite the leaves that constantly
covered the lawn. Sadly over a year we watched as it died, giving
way to old age, perhaps. It now stands as a silhouette against
the hillside. Even in its decay it has a beauty, and we watch in the
mornings as the birds tussle for position on its decaying tips; and
as insects burrow into its trunk the birds burrow after them. We've
discussed planting it with mistletoe, clematis and epiphytic ferns,
and now it's bursting to life with fungi all over its dying wood. With
no help from us its form is springing back to life and I'm fascinated
to see what will happen next as its limbs are reoccupied.

The fungi are key to this process. Within the soil they are as
essential to a plant's wellbeing as the bacteria in our stomachs are

to our digestive processes. A healthy plant's roots are surrounded by beneficial fungi that help balance nutrients and minerals as well as bacteria. Fungi are as essential to good soil as worms are. If you want soil that grows it must be full of life. The good news is that, although fungi are given little attention unless they are on our plates, they are one of the most resilient life forms on the planet.

Worm farms

Worm farms are basically soil factories, and a wonderful way to deal with organic scraps without the bother of rats and possums getting involved. It is important, though, to remember that worms are living creatures to which we gardeners are beholden, and we should take care to keep them in the best condition. They are probably the easiest of pets to maintain. The main thing to watch out for is that conditions do not become too acidic: worms do not love citrus, especially in large amounts.

Like all soil systems, you need to create a balance of brown and green material. Adding layers of leaf litter, straw or newspaper, as well as your kitchen waste will help keep the worms healthy and in balance. If your worm farm (or compost) smells like vinegar it usually means the balance of green to brown is out and you need more brown carbon in your mix. You can add lime to bring down the acidity. If your worm farm looks dry you can add a very small amount of water, but it probably means you are not adding enough green or fresh waste with a high water content to the mix. Alternatively it may be that you are not using your farm regularly enough. If you live on your own, perhaps in a small flat or unit, you may wish to consider inviting others to add to your farm. Increasing the input increases the output, which means more juice to feed the soil.

Worm farms are just one source of liquid fertiliser; seaweed and fish fertilisers are also very valuable in adding nutrients and microbes to the soil. This black gold is a gardener's oil containing the living elements which soil needs to grow.

Bokashi

Bokashi systems are based on traditional Japanese farming techniques that used good, fertile soil high in microorganisms to cover waste and ferment it before burying it directly into the ground. Modern methods involve inoculating untreated sawdust or bran and molasses with microorganisms and mixing these with waste food. This ferments the waste food rather than decomposing it, akin to pickling it. It can then be added to soil where it continues to compost and improve the condition of the soil. The main advantage of bokashi over other composting methods is that it can deal with richer food such as meat and dairy, which are prone to smelling bad when they decompose, giving off gases and attracting flies and rodents which spread disease and can infest good food.

Layers

When adding topsoil or planting mix to an existing substratum, you need to create a bind between the two layers. While in an existing garden cultivating or digging over a soil is not a recommended technique, roughing up the surface of a compacted subsoil before you add to it is really important. This helps to break the surface so that as roots push down into the deeper soil there are cracks that they can push through. Breaking the surface also discourages lazy roots from staying in the richer mix. If the substratum is a heavy clay that has been compacted during construction, you will also need to add gypsum or lime. These break the clay surface and also assist roots to push into the

deeper strata. A soil should always get richer the closer it is to the
surface. Higher levels of organic matter beneath loamier soil can
become anaerobic and turn to putrid gases such as methane. If
you have a very rich volcanic soil you do not need a binding layer
between; you can put a planting mix straight on top, ready to
plant into.

GARDENS IN MODIFIED SOILS

WHEN WE CONSIDER GARDENS WITH MODIFIED SOILS we
often think of adding compost to a healthy garden or potting mix
to a container. But modified soils can also include soils that have
been completely removed and replaced with engineered fill or,
in the most extreme cases, reclamation of land after industry,
landfill or quarrying. These are not circumstances that the average
gardener comes across every day, but as populations increase
these areas are becoming more likely to be reclaimed for housing.
International landscape architect Jihae Hwang of South Korea's
project in Nanjido is an example of where nature is called upon
to restore land that has been decimated. Nanjido was once a low-
lying island on the Han River in Seoul. It was farmed for peanuts
and sorghum, and was an ecological home to wild orchids and
a resting place for migratory birds. The land flooded in periods
of high rainfall, and it was problematic for the local community
but good for the fertility of the land. As Seoul grew and pressures
on the landscape intensified, a dyke was built around the island,
which was designated as a rubbish tip. Over 15 years as growth in
the city continued and its boundaries expanded to reach this once
marginal area, the size of the waste grew into two mountains, each
100 metres high, containing over 92,000 tonnes of waste. If you
think of this in terms of an elephant weighing around 5 tonnes, its

scale truly comes to life. By this point the leaching of methane and other toxins into the surrounding river made clear why positioning a rubbish dump at the heart of a valuable river wasn't a good idea. The waste was so stagnant that the land surrounding it also became contaminated, and the tip itself became the site of fires as methane was released from the decomposing organic matter. During this period there were still over 900 families living in this zone, attempting to make a living from recycling waste products. Their standard of living became increasingly untenable until the methane fires caused the village to burn to the ground. The government closed the tip and looked at ways of dealing with the organic matter, which was the key problem. The decision was made to cover the site in 1 metre of topsoil. Methane that was leaching from beneath was captured and piped from the tip to be used as heating at a nearby stadium and apartment complex.

> The soil quickly came to life with trees, shrubs and wildflowers, and the birds and insects soon followed. It was then decided to turn Nanjido into an ecological park encompassing the surrounding land.

What they didn't expect was how the land was reclaimed. The soil quickly came to life with trees, shrubs and wildflowers, and the birds and insects soon followed. It was then decided to turn Nanjido into an ecological park encompassing the surrounding land. As the organic matter in the site decomposes the land continues to sink and settle, but it has become a shrine to a new way of managing waste. Now organic matter is separated from other materials to be composted and turned into productive soil, and other waste is

carefully sorted and recycled. The park itself is a verdant green space in a very urban environment. Schoolchildren visit to learn about the environment. Jihae Hwan's garden sits within this parkland as a tribute to those who once lived among the poisons in terrible poverty; and it recalls the native plants of the region long lost in the wild. The instability of the soil due to the inorganic matter beneath has in fact given the land and the city new life. The park is now a small island of ecological relief in an increasingly urban world.

PREPARING NEW GROUND

THE INSTABILITY OF A RUBBISH TIP demonstrates the difference between organic matter composted in a method that ensures the pile is well oxygenated and balanced, and organic matter rotting without air. One is a highly valuable product and the other is poisonous. Composting garden and kitchen waste is a relatively simple process and it makes a massive difference to landfills. In Auckland alone, 40 per cent of household waste sent to the tip is compostable.

The instability of the land is also a lesson we gardeners can learn from. As organic matter breaks down, it shrinks. I'm often asked why you should not just build a raised bed over an existing lawn – especially by those who have learned no-till gardening. Several things happen if soil is simply loaded on top.

- If the soil is shallow, then grasses below will simply push through into the lovely top dressing you have just provided; and with established roots systems they will be both difficult to remove and more competitive than newly introduced plants. Invasive plants such as kikuyu will dominate, and attempts to pull it out will result in you pulling your own hair out before long!

- The layer of rotting organic matter beneath your topsoil and the remnant ground can be a problem. If the grass is cut very short before the beds are built this will be minimal, but taller grasses represent a significant biomass, especially when you include the root system, which is often the greater volume of the plants. This will mean that there is an anaerobic layer beneath the surface which can affect soil health.

It also means that as this breaks down your soil is going to sink over time. This often happens with new gardens anyway, but it is increased if you have an organic mass at the base beneath your raised bed. To avoid this you can prepare the ground for planting using carpet or cardboard, which acts as a mulch. While weed-killers were often used last century, modern thinking avoids such unnecessary chemicals wherever possible in favour of cleaner alternatives. The carpet or cardboard allows water to permeate through the surface, unlike a plastic lining. The lack of light and oxygen smothers most plants, which then begin to break down, and when you peel back the carpet or cardboard you should find a vibrant community of life. Worms and other busy insects get hard to work breaking down the organic matter; and there is so much more microbial life that you can't even see with your eye. If the insects are there at work it's a good sign you have a healthy system. Now, when you layer the earth on top, that healthy soil system will make its way to the top of the new garden.

Another technique is to simply use layers of organic brown carbon thickly piled up on the area you plan to prepare. This could be leaves collected in the autumn, or hedge prunings. Lawn clippings are too green and can only be used as a mulch in thin layers, or they fire up to high temperatures and become a breeding ground for flies and the like. They are also more acidic. The brown carbon, though, will have a similar effect to carpet or newspaper, and can be redistributed into the garden as a mulch once the ground is prepared.

SOILS IN THE SKY

THE HIGH LINE PARK IN NEW YORK tells another story of soil and plants reclaiming a cityscape. This now-famous garden sits upon an old railway line that was built floating above the streetscape below. The line was abandoned as the lie of the city changed over years and was left sitting, an abandoned stretch of steel in the sky, winding through an industrial and poorer part of the city. Had it been elsewhere the social pressure to remove such a structure might have seen it pulled down years before for scrap, and had it been in a poorer part of the world it perhaps would have been pillaged by looters or occupied as a shanty town.

As dust and debris collected, over decades a thin crust of topsoil began to form between the remnant tracks. And where there is soil, the plants soon follow. The diversity of life that fell on these tracks began to attract the attention of those who notice such things, including Joshua David and Peter Hammond, who lived in the High Line neighbourhood. Seeds must have arrived via winds and birds, and those that survived created a new and distinct ecology. Before the tracks were developed, nature had reclaimed this area as a green space. The residents gathered together to formalise its status and develop it further into what is now New York's second most famous park. The tracks remain through drifts of planting designed by the influential Dutch garden designer Piet Oudolf, as do odes to the graffiti which once decorated the area,

which is now immortalised in twisted, rust-stained signatures silhouetted against the sky.

Soil not only instigated this project, it was also a defining factor in how spaces could be planted and the form they may take. A good organic soil is very heavy when loaded with water, so mixes need to be custom designed to contain low-weight gravels that allow water to drain away freely. A similar approach is taken with roof gardens in other parts of the world, such as London, where new buildings are often required to have green roofs to comply with environmental standards. A developer is given greater incentives if they can also make use of demolition materials such as crushed bricks on a site to form part of the soil medium used in these 'floating' roof gardens.

> A good organic soil is very heavy when loaded with water, so mixes need to be custom-designed to contain low-weight gravels that allow water to drain away freely.

Obviously trees require a greater depth of soil, so areas where trees were placed needed to be able to carry a heavier loading. The distinctive prairie plantings of Oudolf are perfect in a rooftop garden; the species are selected for their preference for gravelly soils and their ability to grow in shallow beds. This shows the diversity of these plants that in a normal setting would have roots that would hang through the old rail tracks, creating a curtain above the busy streets below. But plant roots follow the nutrients and water, and if there is enough flowing they will thrive on shallow ground or, if needed, grow deep to draw the water up.

INGREDIENTS GUIDE

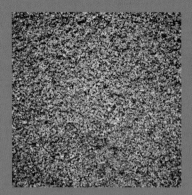

PUMICE SAND

Great to keep mixes free-draining. Its porous nature means water can flow through but soil still retains nutrients and microorganisms.

COMPOST

The food of our soils. It can condition existing beds that need improvement, or it can be combined with other media to create a balanced planting mix.

BARK MEDIUM

Provides a good base for potting media for consistency of water retention and even distribution of nutrients.

COCONUT FIBRE

Light, and has excellent water retention qualities.

WETTING AGENT

Ensures that water moves evenly through a mix and that a mix does not become heavily saturated.

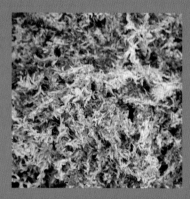

SPHAGNUM MOSS

Ideal for hanging baskets or containers that need low soil content as it retains water and nutrients.

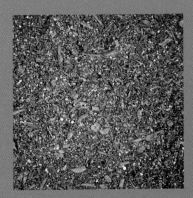

SLOW-RELEASE FERTILISER

Ideal when soil volumes are limited, such as in pots or planters. Allows an even release of nutrients over time in artificial circumstances.

SCORIA

This rock is porous, so is ideal where drainage is needed. Water flows through the stone easily, improving drainage.

TERRACOTTA

A porous material that assists with drainage. This lets air and water into a soil.

MULCH

Important in reducing oxidisation which occurs when a soil is left exposed. Protects beneficial bacteria, fungi and worms in new gardens.

PLANTING APPROACH

When working above ground, drainage is of most importance. Make sure you consider water run-off from pots or planters and the ongoing effects of any run-off. This applies especially to pots on timber surfaces.

Where soil is limited you need to take more care with feeding. This can be done with slow-release fertilisers and should not be neglected.

Plants in pots will need repotting over time. If a plant is starting to look stressed and has adequate fertiliser and water it is probably time for a larger container.

Annuals in pots still use up organic matter so your potting mix will become depleted over time and need replacing. You can replace half the mix at a time, though this will mean there is less fertiliser in the mix. If mix is very root-bound, use it to mulch shrubs in the garden and replace the whole mix.

Pots do dry out and the roots will have no water table to depend on, so if you have a container garden you need to commit to watering or install an irrigation system.

Index

Acknowledgements

Thank you to the friends and designers who, with absolute generosity, have placed their work into my hands to use as I wish. It is with such gratitude that I am able to share these pages with you all. I greatly admire not only the beauty of your work but also the intelligence and sensitivity that you all maintain towards both plants and the earth upon which you work.

Thank you James and Helen Basson, Andrew Wilson, Gavin McWilliam, Peter Macdonald, Steve Martino, Diana Wiesner, Jihae Hwang, Yosuke Yamaguchi san, Thomas Doxiadis, Nuno Almeida, Gary Marshall, Zoe Carafice, James Walkinshaw, Natasha Iyer, Rajendra Thakkar, Kate Grace and Andy Hamilton.

To the editorial team, Debra Millar and Abby Aitcheson, who pulled the multiple threads together to complete this book.

To the artful gardeners who have spent years mastering mother earth, for sharing their work with us all and helping me to continue learning: Bev McConnell, Amanda and Phip Rinaldo, Sally McKibbin, Lesley Dunn and Anthony Viner, Rob and Martha Wagoner amongst others.

To Daltons for their help with soil media and especially to Judith and Daltons Plantation for the lessons this garden allows me to continue to learn, but most importantly for your friendship.

To my dear friend Jessie Casson, who made completing the photography a mix of delightful adventures and fabulous lunches.

To the community of creatives, makers, friends, clients and plants people who I have the privilege of working with or learning from: Justin Hurt, Katrina Christison, James Walkinshaw, Zoe Carafice, Terry, Pat and Lindsay Hatch, Rowena Price, Geoff Davidson, Natasha Iyer, Sophie Dungate, Evan Veza, Adam Evans, Yue Yu, Claire Mahoney, Mitsuo Takatori, Selgum Savitha, Helen and James Basson, Anya Brighouse and Ru Wilkie.

To Gillian Monahan, who reminded me to look up and out as well as down.

My children, Jacob and Sophie Lee, these words are for you and for the world I want you to grow old in. My parents, David and Judy, my brother Clement, these words are from you and the world you shared with me; thank you for this koha, this taonga. To Tony, Jan, Lesley and Anthony, for the support they maintain around us.

To Christopher and Flit, our shared joy, gratitude and ambitions that enrich two paths woven together to build a strong kete, to carry forth future generations into the unknown.

Image Credits